A ARTE DE CONJUGAR

Verbos Ingleses

de
Samantha Scott

Tradução
MONICA STAHEL

wmf martinsfontes

SÃO PAULO 2015

1ª edição *2001*
2ª edição *2009*
3ª tiragem *2015*

Tradução
MONICA STAHEL

Revisão gráfica
Ana Maria de Oliveira Mendes Barbosa
Sandra Regina de Souza
Produção gráfica
Geraldo Alves
Paginação/Fotolitos
Studio 3 Desenvolvimento Editorial

Dados Internacionais de Catalogação na Publicação (CIP)
(Câmara Brasileira do Livro, SP, Brasil)

Scott, Samantha
A arte de conjugar verbos ingleses / de Samantha Scott ; tradução Monica Stahel. – 2ª ed. – São Paulo : Editora WMF Martins Fontes, 2009.

Título original: Verbtabellen Englisch.
ISBN 978-85-7827-114-5

1. Inglês – Verbos I. Título.

09-01862 CDD-425

Índices para catálogo sistemático:
1. Verbos : Inglês : Linguística 425

Editora WMF Martins Fontes Ltda.
Rua Prof. Laerte Ramos de Carvalho, 133 01325.030 São Paulo SP Brasil
Tel. (11) 3293.8150 Fax (11) 3101.1042
e-mail: info@wmfmartinsfontes.com.br http://www.wmfmartinsfontes.com.br

Sumário

Como utilizar este livro

Este livro pode ser utilizado por quem deseja conhecer e fixar as formas de um determinado verbo e, ao mesmo tempo, informar-se sobre suas particularidades e irregularidades. Também pode ser utilizado para consultas rápidas, quando se apresenta alguma dúvida sobre o emprego de uma determinada forma verbal.

A arte de conjugar verbos ingleses lhe oferece **tabelas de conjugação** de 84 verbos regulares e irregulares. Esses modelos de conjugação mostram todas as formas – inclusive as compostas – numa mesma página, facilitando a consulta e a visualização. As particularidades de cada verbo são grafadas em cores e resumidas em fórmulas práticas, colocadas no alto da respectiva tabela de conjugação.

Construção das tabelas de conjugação

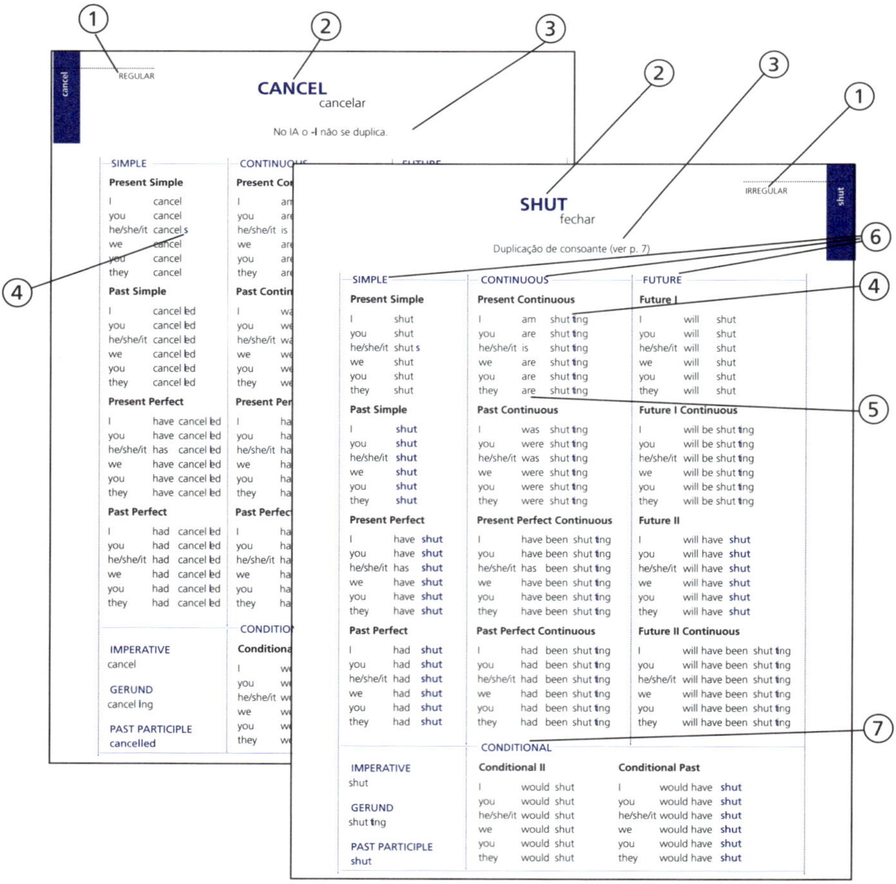

① **Número da tabela:** Identificação da posição de cada verbo na lista por ordem alfabética.

② **Verbo e tradução:** Identificação do verbo conjugado com sua tradução para o português.

③ **Características:** Indicação das particularidades ou irregularidades do verbo.

④ **Destaque em cores:** As formas que divergem da conjugação regular ou as particularidades da língua inglesa (p. ex., 3ª pessoa do singular do *Present Simple* **-s**) são grafadas em **azul**.

⑤ **Omissão das formas abreviadas:** Nas tabelas de conjugação o verbo auxiliar é sempre apresentado em sua forma escrita. O emprego da forma coloquial abreviada é apresentado na p. 9.

⑥ **Disposição da tabela:** Na coluna da esquerda estão as formas simples dos verbos, na coluna do meio as formas do passado e na coluna da direita as formas do futuro.

⑦ **Condicional:** Como o *Conditional I* e o *Future I* são construídos de maneira idêntica, a apresentação do *Conditional I* foi deliberadamente omitida.

Na **lista dos verbos ingleses irregulares** no final deste livro você encontrará 100 dos verbos irregulares mais usados. Na última página há um índice português-inglês, em ordem alfabética, do qual constam todos os verbos conjugados neste livro com a indicação da página em que se encontra cada um deles.

Atenção: no cabeçalho de cada tabela você encontrará várias informações importantes sobre o verbo conjugado. Nas páginas 7 e 8 há uma série de observações sistematizadas sobre **particularidades ortográficas** e **indicações de pronúncia.** Na página 10 apresentam-se os **pronomes reflexivos**. E na página 11 apresentam-se indicações breves e precisas sobre o **emprego dos tempos verbais**.
Bom proveito!

Observações sobre ortografia

Os verbos em inglês podem ter as seguintes terminações:

1. **Verbo + *-s / -es***
2. **Verbo + *-ed / -d / -ied***
3. **Verbo + *-ing***

No entanto, alguns verbos sofrem alterações ortográficas.

1. Verbo + *-s / -es*

para a 3ª pessoa da singular do *Present Simple*

verbos terminados em *-ch, -sh, -ss, -o, -x*	acréscimo de *-es*	watch push go	watch**es** push**es** go**es**
verbos terminados em consoante + *-y*	acréscimo de *-ies* eliminação do *-y*	study try carry	stud**ies** tr**ies** carr**ies**
mas: verbos terminados em vogal + *-y*	Acréscimo de *-s*	play buy enjoy	play**s** buy**s** enjoy**s**

2. Verbo + *-ed / -d / -ied*

Nos verbos regulares a terminação *-ed* é acrescentada para formar o *Past Simple* e o *Past Participle.*

verbos terminados em *-e*	acréscimo de *-d*	arrive change	arrive**d** change**d**
verbos terminados em consoante + *-y*	*-y* é substituído por *-ied*	carry try study	carr**ied** tr**ied** stud**ied**
verbos terminados em uma vogal e uma consoante	a consoante é duplicada	stop plan	stop**ped** plan**ned**
verbos dissílabos terminados em uma consoante	consoante só se duplica quando a última sílaba é tônica	prefer *mas* visit offer	prefer**red** visit**ed** offer**ed**

EXCEÇÃO – no IB o *-l* final também é duplicado quando a última sílaba é átona. No IA isso não ocorre. Exemplo: travel travelled (IB)
travel traveled (IA)

3. Verbo + *-ing*

A terminação *-ing* é utilizada para o *Gerund* e o *Present Participle.*

verbos terminados em *-e*	eliminação do *-e* acréscimo de *-ing*	have dance	hav**ing** danc**ing**
verbos terminados em *-ee*	acréscimo de *-ing*	see	see**ing**
verbos cuja consoante final é tônica e precedida de uma vogal	duplicação da consoante	stop plan get begin	stop**ping** plan**ning** get**ting** begin**ning**
EXCEÇÃO – No IB o *-l* final precedido de uma vogal também é duplicado quando a última sílaba é átona: cancel cancelling (IB) cancel canceling (IA)			

Pronúncia

Pronúncia do *-ed* no *Past Simple* e no *Past Participle*

A terminação *-ed* é pronunciada:

depois de consoante surda (depois de *-p, -f, -ss* etc.)	(**-t**) surdo	asked looked stopped	como t em aspecto p. ex. [ɑːskt]
depois de consoantes e vogais sonoras (depois de *-b, -v, -g* etc.)	(**-d**) sonoro	allowed listened opened	como d em "comendo" p. ex. ['əʊpənd]
depois de *-d* e *-t*	(**-id**) sibilante	needed waited wanted	como id em "vide" p. ex. ['niːdɪd]

Pronúncia do *-s* na 3ª pessoa do singular do *Present Simple*

A terminação *-s* é pronunciada:

depois de consoante surda	(**-s**) surdo*	waits gets cuts	como ss em "massa" p. ex. [gets]
depois de vogais e consoantes sonoras	(**-z**) sonoro*	runs opens allows	como s em "casa" p. ex. [rʌnz]
depois de uma letra sibilante, na 3ª pessoa do sing. do *Present Simple*	(**-iz**) sibilante	changes watches washes	como s de "poesia" p. ex. ['wɒʃɪz]

* Há dois tipos de consoantes em inglês
consoante sonora: há uma vibração na laringe.
consoante surda: não há vibração na laringe.

Formas abreviadas

As formas abreviadas dos verbos são usadas na linguagem coloquial. Na linguagem escrita formal usam-se as formas completas.

BE		
I am	→	I'm
you are	→	you're
he / she / it is	→	he's / she's / it's
we are	→	we're
you are	→	you're
they are	→	they're

HAVE		
I have	→	I've
you have	→	you've
he / she / it has	→	he's / she's / it's
we have	→	we've
you have	→	you've
they have	→	they've

HAD		
I had	→	I'd
you had	→	you'd
he / she / it had	→	he'd / she'd / it'd
we had	→	we'd
you had	→	you'd
they had	→	they'd

WILL		
I will	→	I'll
you will	→	you'll
he / she / it	→	he'll / she'll / it'll
we will	→	we'll
you will	→	you'll
they will	→	they'll

WOULD		
I would	→	I'd
you would	→	you'd
he / she / it would	→	he'd / she'd / it'd
we would	→	we'd
you would	→	you'd
they would	→	they'd

Pronomes reflexivos

As formas utilizadas em inglês para indicar que a ação reverte sobre o próprio sujeito são *myself, yourself, himself*, e assim por diante, correspondendo em português aos pronomes me, te, se etc.

I	enjoy	**myself**	we	enjoy	**ourselves**
you	enjoy	**yourself**	you	enjoy	**yourselves**
he	enjoys	**himself**	they	enjoy	**themselves**
she	enjoys	**herself**			
it	enjoys	**itself**			

Tempos verbais

Em inglês há 14 tempos verbais. Há os tempos de *Simple Form* (forma simples) e *Continuous Form* (forma contínua).

A **Simple Form** é empregada para
- ações ou estados regulares ou repetitivos
- fatos
- estados de duração ilimitada

A **Continuous Form** é empregada para
- ações que estão ou estavam se desenrolando num determinado momento
- uma ação que acaba de ocorrer na qual se encadeia uma outra ação
- duas ações que ocorrem paralelamente.

Há alguns verbos que não podem ser conjugados na forma contínua, como por exemplo: *like, hope, know, love.*

Present Simple

O *Present Simple* se constrói com o *Infinitive*. Só se altera na 3ª pessoa do singular (*he / she / it*), em que se acrescenta um *-s*.

Afirmativa		**Negativa**			**Interrogativa**		
I / we / you / they	live.	I / we / you / they	do not (don't)	live.	Do	I / we / you / they	live?
he / she / it	lives.	he / she / it	does not (doesn't)	live.	Does	he / she / it	live?
		A forma negativa se constrói com *do not* (don't) / *does not* (doesn't) entre o sujeito e o verbo no *Infinitive*.			A forma interrogativa se constrói com *do / does* antes do sujeito + o verbo no *Infinitive*.		

Present Simple Continuous

O *Present Simple Continuous* se constrói com a forma do presente de *to be* (*is / am / are*) + o *Gerund* (*Infinitive + -ing*).

Afirmativa			**Negativa**			**Interrogativa**		
I	am	living.	I	am not ('m not)	living.	Am	I	living?
he / she / it	is	living.	he /she / it	is not ('s not)	living.	Is	he / she / it	living?
we / you / they	are	living.	we / you / they	are not ('re not)	living.	Are	we / you / they	living?
			A forma negativa se constrói acrescentando *not* entre o verbo *to be* e o verbo principal.			A forma interrogativa se constrói deslocando *am / is / are* para antes do sujeito.		

Past Simple

O *Past Simple* é formado acrescentando-se *-ed* ao *Infinitive*. Há uma lista de verbos irregulares nas pp. 101-103.

Afirmativa		**Negativa**			**Interrogativa**		
I	lived.	I	did not	live.	Did	I	live?
he / she / it		he / she / it	(didn't)			he / she / it	
we / you / they		we / you / they				we / you / they	
		A forma negativa é construída com (*didn't*) + o *Infinitive*.			A forma interrogativa se constrói com *did* antes do sujeito + o *Infinitive* (*did* é o *Past Simple de do / does*).		

Atenção: o *Past Simple* refere-se a ações que não se prolongam no presente.

Past Continuous

O *Past Continuous* se constrói com *was / were* + o *Gerund* (*Infinitive* + *-ing*)

Afirmativa			**Negativa**			**Interrogativa**		
I / he / she / it	was	living.	I / he / she / it	was not	living.	Was	I / he / she / it	living?
we / you / they	were	living.	we / you / they	were not	living.	Were	we / you / they	living?
			A forma negativa se constrói com a inclusão de *not* depois de *was* ou *were*.			A forma interrogativa se constrói deslocando *was* ou *were* para antes do sujeito.		

Present Perfect

O *Present Perfect* se constrói com *have / has* + *Past Participle* (terceira forma do verbo).
O *Past Participle* dos verbos regulares é formado acrescentando-se *-ed* ao *Infinitive*.
As formas irregulares são encontradas às pp. 101-103.

Afirmativa			**Negativa**			**Interrogativa**		
I / we / you / they	have	lived.	I / we / you / they	have not (haven't)	lived.	Have	I / we / you / they	lived?
he / she / it	has	lived.	he / she / it	has not (hasn't)	lived.	Has	he / she / it	lived?
			A forma negativa se constrói com a inclusão de *not* antes do *Past Participle*.			A forma interrogativa se constrói deslocando-se *have / has* para antes do sujeito.		

Atenção: O *Present Perfect* se distingue do *Past Simple* por ter uma relação com o presente. Ele estabelece uma ponte entre o passado e o presente.

Present Perfect Continuous

O *Present Perfect Continuous* se constrói com *have been / has been* + o *Gerund* (*Infinitive* + *-ing*).

Afirmativa			Negativa			Interrogativa		
I / we / you / they	have	been living.	I / we / you / they	have not (haven't)	been living.	Have	I / we / you / they	been living?
he / she / it	has	been living.	he / she / it	has not (hasn't)	been living.	Has	he / she / it	been living?
			A forma negativa se constrói com *not* entre *have / has* e *been*.			A forma interrogativa se constrói deslocando *have / has* para antes do sujeito.		

Past Perfect

O *Past Perfect* se constrói com *had* + o *Past Participle* do verbo. Nos verbos regulares, o *Past Participle* se constrói pelo acréscimo de *-ed* ao *Infinitive*. As formas irregulares encontram-se nas pp. 101-103.

Afirmativa			Negativa			Interrogativa		
I	had	lived.	I	had not (hadn't)	lived.	Had	I	lived?
he / she / it			he /she / it				he / she / it	
we / you / they			we / you / they				we / you / they	
			A forma negativa se constrói com *not* depois de *had*.			A forma interrogativa se constrói deslocando *had* para antes do sujeito.		

Past Perfect Continuous

O *Past Perfect Continuous* se constrói com *had been* + o *Gerund* do verbo (*Infinitive* + *-ing*).

Afirmativa			Negativa			Interrogativa		
I	had	been living.	I	had not (hadn't)	been living.	Had	I	been living?
he / she / it			he / she / it				he /she / it	
we / you / they			we / you / they				we / you / they	
			A forma negativa se constrói com a inclusão de *not* entre *had* e *been*.			A forma interrogativa se constrói deslocando *had* para antes do sujeito.		

Future I

O *Future I* se constrói com *will* + o *Infinitive* do verbo.

<table>
<tr><th colspan="3">Afirmativa</th><th colspan="3">Negativa</th><th colspan="3">Interrogativa</th></tr>
<tr><td>I</td><td rowspan="3">will</td><td rowspan="3">live.</td><td>I</td><td rowspan="3">will not
(won't)</td><td rowspan="3">live.</td><td rowspan="3">Will</td><td>I</td><td rowspan="3">live?</td></tr>
<tr><td>he / she / it</td><td>he / she / it</td><td>he / she / it</td></tr>
<tr><td>we / you / they</td><td>we / you / they</td><td>we / you / they</td></tr>
<tr><td colspan="3"></td><td colspan="3">A forma negativa se constrói com a inclusão de not entre will e o Infinitive do verbo.
Atenção: forma abreviada → won't</td><td colspan="3">A forma interrogativa se constrói deslocando will para antes do sujeito.</td></tr>
</table>

Future I Continuous

O *Future I Continuous* se constrói com *will be* + o *Gerund* do verbo.

<table>
<tr><th colspan="3">Afirmativa</th><th colspan="3">Negativa</th><th colspan="3">Interrogativa</th></tr>
<tr><td>I</td><td rowspan="3">will be</td><td rowspan="3">living.</td><td>I</td><td rowspan="3">will not be
(won't)</td><td rowspan="3">living.</td><td rowspan="3">Will</td><td>I</td><td rowspan="3">be
living?</td></tr>
<tr><td>he / she / it</td><td>he / she / it</td><td>he / she / it</td></tr>
<tr><td>we / you / they</td><td>we / you / they</td><td>we / you / they</td></tr>
<tr><td colspan="3"></td><td colspan="3">A forma negativa se constrói com a inclusão de not entre will e be.</td><td colspan="3">A forma interrogativa se constrói deslocando will para antes do sujeito.</td></tr>
</table>

Future II

O *Future II* se constrói com *will have* + o *Past Participle* do verbo.

<table>
<tr><th colspan="3">Afirmativa</th><th colspan="3">Negativa</th><th colspan="3">Interrogativa</th></tr>
<tr><td>I</td><td rowspan="3">will
have</td><td rowspan="3">lived.</td><td>I</td><td rowspan="3">will not have
(won't)</td><td rowspan="3">lived.</td><td rowspan="3">Will</td><td>I</td><td rowspan="3">have
lived?</td></tr>
<tr><td>he / she / it</td><td>he / she / it</td><td>he / she / it</td></tr>
<tr><td>we / you / they</td><td>we / you / they</td><td>we / you / they</td></tr>
<tr><td colspan="3"></td><td colspan="3">A forma negativa se constrói com a inclusão de not entre will e have.</td><td colspan="3">A forma interrogativa se constrói deslocando will para antes do sujeito.</td></tr>
</table>

Future II Continuous

O *Future II Continuous* se constrói com *will have been* + o *Gerund* do verbo.

Afirmativa		
I	will	living.
he / she / it	have	
we / you / they	been	

Negativa		
I	will not have been	living.
he / she / it	(won't)	
we / you / they		

A forma negativa se constrói com a inclusão de *not* entre *will* e *have*.

Interrogativa		
Will	I	have
	he / she / it	been
	we / you / they	living?

A forma interrogativa se constrói deslocando *will* para antes do sujeito.

Conditional II

O *Conditional II* se constrói com *would* + o *Infinitive* do verbo.

Afirmativa		
I	would	live.
he / she / it		
we / you / they		

Negativa		
I	would not	live.
he / she / it	(wouldn't)	
we / you / they		

A forma negativa se constrói com a inclusão de *not* depois de *would*.

Interrogativa		
Would	I	live?
	he / she / it	
	we / you / they	

A forma interrogativa se constrói deslocando *would* para antes do sujeito.

Conditional Past

O *Conditional past* se constrói com *would have* + o *Infinitive* do verbo.

Afirmativa		
I	would	lived.
he / she / it	have	
we / you / they		

Negativa		
I	would not have	lived.
he / she / it	(wouldn't)	
we / you / they		

A forma negativa se constrói com a inclusão de *not* entre *would* e *have*.

Interrogativa		
Would	I	have
	he / she / it	lived?
	we / you / they	

A forma interrogativa se constrói deslocando *would* para antes do sujeito.

Passiv
Voz passiva

A voz passiva se constrói com o verbo *to be* (*is / was / has been* etc.) e o *Past Participle* (*clean / done / sold* etc.).

SIMPLE

Present Simple

I	am	taught
you	are	taught
he/she/it	is	taught
we	are	taught
you	are	taught
they	are	taught

Past Simple

I	was	taught
you	were	taught
he/she/it	was	taught
we	were	taught
you	were	taught
they	were	taught

Present Perfect

I	have been	taught
you	have been	taught
he/she/it	has been	taught
we	have been	taught
you	have been	taught
they	have been	taught

Past Perfect

I	had	been taught
you	had	been taught
he/she/it	had	been taught
we	had	been taught
you	had	been taught
they	had	been taught

CONTINUOUS

Present Continuous

I	am	being taught
you	are	being taught
he/she/it	is	being taught
we	are	being taught
you	are	being taught
they	are	being taught

Past Continuous

I	was	being taught
you	were	being taught
he/she/it	was	being taught
we	were	being taught
you	were	being taught
they	were	being taught

Present Perfect Continuous

I	have	been being taught
you	have	been being taught
he/she/it	has	been being taught
we	have	been being taught
you	have	been being taught
they	have	been being taught

Past Perfect Continuous

I	had	been being taught
you	had	been being taught
he/she/it	had	been being taught
we	had	been being taught
you	had	been being taught
they	had	been being taught

FUTURE

Future I

I	will	be taught
you	will	be taught
he/she/it	will	be taught
we	will	be taught
you	will	be taught
they	will	be taught

Future I Continuous

I	will be	being taught
you	will be	being taught
he/she/it	will be	being taught
we	will be	being taught
you	will be	being taught
they	will be	being taught

Future II

I	will have	been taught
you	will have	been taught
he/she/it	will have	been taught
we	will have	been taught
you	will have	been taught
they	will have	been taught

Future II Continuous

I	will have been	being taught
you	will have been	being taught
he/she/it	will have been	being taught
we	will have been	being taught
you	will have been	being taught
they	will have been	being taught

IMPERATIVE

be + Past Participle*

GERUND

being taught

CONDITIONAL

Conditional II

I	would	be taught
you	would	be taught
he/she/it	would	be taught
we	would	be taught
you	would	be taught
they	would	be taught

Conditional Past

I	would have	been taught
you	would have	been taught
he/she/it	would have	been taught
we	would have	been taught
you	would have	been taught
they	would have	been taught

* raro

ALLOW
permitir

SIMPLE

Present Simple

I	allow
you	allow
he/she/it	allows
we	allow
you	allow
they	allow

Past Simple

I	allowed
you	allowed
he/she/it	allowed
we	allowed
you	allowed
they	allowed

Present Perfect

I	have	allowed
you	have	allowed
he/she/it	has	allowed
we	have	allowed
you	have	allowed
they	have	allowed

Past Perfect

I	had	allowed
you	had	allowed
he/she/it	had	allowed
we	had	allowed
you	had	allowed
they	had	allowed

CONTINUOUS

Present Continuous

I	am	allowing
you	are	allowing
he/she/it	is	allowing
we	are	allowing
you	are	allowing
they	are	allowing

Past Continuous

I	was	allowing
you	were	allowing
he/she/it	was	allowing
we	were	allowing
you	were	allowing
they	were	allowing

Present Perfect Continuous

I	have been	allowing
you	have been	allowing
he/she/it	has been	allowing
we	have been	allowing
you	have been	allowing
they	have been	allowing

Past Perfect Continuous

I	had been	allowing
you	had been	allowing
he/she/it	had been	allowing
we	had been	allowing
you	had been	allowing
they	had been	allowing

FUTURE

Future I

I	will	allow
you	will	allow
he/she/it	will	allow
we	will	allow
you	will	allow
they	will	allow

Future I Continuous

I	will be allowing
you	will be allowing
he/she/it	will be allowing
we	will be allowing
you	will be allowing
they	will be allowing

Future II

I	will have allowed
you	will have allowed
he/she/it	will have allowed
we	will have allowed
you	will have allowed
they	will have allowed

Future II Continuous

I	will have been	allowing
you	will have been	allowing
he/she/it	will have been	allowing
we	will have been	allowing
you	will have been	allowing
they	will have been	allowing

IMPERATIVE
allow

GERUND
allowing

PAST PARTICIPLE
allowed

CONDITIONAL

Conditional II

I	would	allow
you	would	allow
he/she/it	would	allow
we	would	allow
you	would	allow
they	would	allow

Conditional Past

I	would have	allowed
you	would have	allowed
he/she/it	would have	allowed
we	would have	allowed
you	would have	allowed
they	would have	allowed

REGULAR

ANSWER
responder

SIMPLE

Present Simple

I	answer
you	answer
he/she/it	answers
we	answer
you	answer
they	answer

Past Simple

I	answered
you	answered
he/she/it	answered
we	answered
you	answered
they	answered

Present Perfect

I	have	answered
you	have	answered
he/she/it	has	answered
we	have	answered
you	have	answered
they	have	answered

Past Perfect

I	had	answered
you	had	answered
he/she/it	had	answered
we	had	answered
you	had	answered
they	had	answered

CONTINUOUS

Present Continuous

I	am	answering
you	are	answering
he/she/it	is	answering
we	are	answering
you	are	answering
they	are	answering

Past Continuous

I	was	answering
you	were	answering
he/she/it	was	answering
we	were	answering
you	were	answering
they	were	answering

Present Perfect Continuous

I	have	been	answering
you	have	been	answering
he/she/it	has	been	answering
we	have	been	answering
you	have	been	answering
they	have	been	answering

Past Perfect Continuous

I	had	been	answering
you	had	been	answering
he/she/it	had	been	answering
we	had	been	answering
you	had	been	answering
they	had	been	answering

FUTURE

Future I

I	will	answer
you	will	answer
he/she/it	will	answer
we	will	answer
you	will	answer
they	will	answer

Future I Continuous

I	will be answering
you	will be answering
he/she/it	will be answering
we	will be answering
you	will be answering
they	will be answering

Future II

I	will have answered
you	will have answered
he/she/it	will have answered
we	will have answered
you	will have answered
they	will have answered

Future II Continuous

I	will have been	answering
you	will have been	answering
he/she/it	will have been	answering
we	will have been	answering
you	will have been	answering
they	will have been	answering

IMPERATIVE
answer

GERUND
answering

PAST PARTICIPLE
answered

CONDITIONAL

Conditional II

I	would	answer
you	would	answer
he/she/it	would	answer
we	would	answer
you	would	answer
they	would	answer

Conditional Past

I	would have	answered
you	would have	answered
he/she/it	would have	answered
we	would have	answered
you	would have	answered
they	would have	answered

ARRIVE
chegar

+ *-ing* → ~~e~~ (ver p. 8) / + *-d* não *-ed* (ver p. 7)

SIMPLE

Present Simple

I	arrive
you	arrive
he/she/it	arrives
we	arrive
you	arrive
they	arrive

Past Simple

I	arrived
you	arrived
he/she/it	arrived
we	arrived
you	arrived
they	arrived

Present Perfect

I	have	arrived
you	have	arrived
he/she/it	has	arrived
we	have	arrived
you	have	arrived
they	have	arrived

Past Perfect

I	had	arrived
you	had	arrived
he/she/it	had	arrived
we	had	arrived
you	had	arrived
they	had	arrived

CONTINUOUS

Present Continuous

I	am	arriving
you	are	arriving
he/she/it	is	arriving
we	are	arriving
you	are	arriving
they	are	arriving

Past Continuous

I	was	arriving
you	were	arriving
he/she/it	was	arriving
we	were	arriving
you	were	arriving
they	were	arriving

Present Perfect Continuous

I	have been	arriving
you	have been	arriving
he/she/it	has been	arriving
we	have been	arriving
you	have been	arriving
they	have been	arriving

Past Perfect Continuous

I	had been	arriving
you	had been	arriving
he/she/it	had been	arriving
we	had been	arriving
you	had been	arriving
they	had been	arriving

FUTURE

Future I

I	will	arrive
you	will	arrive
he/she/it	will	arrive
we	will	arrive
you	will	arrive
they	will	arrive

Future I Continuous

I	will be arriving
you	will be arriving
he/she/it	will be arriving
we	will be arriving
you	will be arriving
they	will be arriving

Future II

I	will have	arrived
you	will have	arrived
he/she/it	will have	arrived
we	will have	arrived
you	will have	arrived
they	will have	arrived

Future II Continuous

I	will have been	arriving
you	will have been	arriving
he/she/it	will have been	arriving
we	will have been	arriving
you	will have been	arriving
they	will have been	arriving

IMPERATIVE
arrive

GERUND
arriving

PAST PARTICIPLE
arrived

CONDITIONAL

Conditional II

I	would	arrive
you	would	arrive
he/she/it	would	arrive
we	would	arrive
you	would	arrive
they	would	arrive

Conditional Past

I	would have	arrived
you	would have	arrived
he/she/it	would have	arrived
we	would have	arrived
you	would have	arrived
they	would have	arrived

ASK

pedir, perguntar

SIMPLE

Present Simple

I	ask
you	ask
he/she/it	asks
we	ask
you	ask
they	ask

Past Simple

I	asked
you	asked
he/she/it	asked
we	asked
you	asked
they	asked

Present Perfect

I	have	asked
you	have	asked
he/she/it	has	asked
we	have	asked
you	have	asked
they	have	asked

Past Perfect

I	had	asked
you	had	asked
he/she/it	had	asked
we	had	asked
you	had	asked
they	had	asked

CONTINUOUS

Present Continuous

I	am	asking
you	are	asking
he/she/it	is	asking
we	are	asking
you	are	asking
they	are	asking

Past Continuous

I	was	asking
you	were	asking
he/she/it	was	asking
we	were	asking
you	were	asking
they	were	asking

Present Perfect Continuous

I	have been	asking
you	have been	asking
he/she/it	has been	asking
we	have been	asking
you	have been	asking
they	have been	asking

Past Perfect Continuous

I	had been	asking
you	had been	asking
he/she/it	had been	asking
we	had been	asking
you	had been	asking
they	had been	asking

FUTURE

Future I

I	will	ask
you	will	ask
he/she/it	will	ask
we	will	ask
you	will	ask
they	will	ask

Future I Continuous

I	will be asking
you	will be asking
he/she/it	will be asking
we	will be asking
you	will be asking
they	will be asking

Future II

I	will have	asked
you	will have	asked
he/she/it	will have	asked
we	will have	asked
you	will have	asked
they	will have	asked

Future II Continuous

I	will have been	asking
you	will have been	asking
he/she/it	will have been	asking
we	will have been	asking
you	will have been	asking
they	will have been	asking

IMPERATIVE

ask

GERUND

asking

PAST PARTICIPLE

asked

CONDITIONAL

Conditional II

I	would	ask
you	would	ask
he/she/it	would	ask
we	would	ask
you	would	ask
they	would	ask

Conditional Past

I	would have	asked
you	would have	asked
he/she/it	would have	asked
we	would have	asked
you	would have	asked
they	would have	asked

IRREGULAR
TAMBÉM VERBO AUXILIAR

BE

ser, estar

O verbo *to be* é utilizado na construção da voz passiva.

SIMPLE

Present Simple

I	am
you	are
he/she/it	is
we	are
you	are
they	are

Past Simple

I	was
you	were
he/she/it	was
we	were
you	were
they	were

Present Perfect

I	have	been
you	have	been
he/she/it	has	been
we	have	been
you	have	been
they	have	been

Past Perfect

I	had	been
you	had	been
he/she/it	had	been
we	had	been
you	had	been
they	had	been

CONTINUOUS

Present Continuous

I	am	being
you	are	being
he/she/it	is	being
we	are	being
you	are	being
they	are	being

Past Continuous

I	was	being
you	were	being
he/she/it	was	being
we	were	being
you	were	being
they	were	being

Present Perfect Continuous

I	have been	being
you	have been	being
he/she/it	has been	being
we	have been	being
you	have been	being
they	have been	being

Past Perfect Continuous

I	had been	being
you	had been	being
he/she/it	had been	being
we	had been	being
you	had been	being
they	had been	being

FUTURE

Future I

I	will	be
you	will	be
he/she/it	will	be
we	will	be
you	will	be
they	will	be

Future I Continuous

I	will be being
you	will be being
he/she/it	will be being
we	will be being
you	will be being
they	will be being

Future II

I	will have	been
you	will have	been
he/she/it	will have	been
we	will have	been
you	will have	been
they	will have	been

Future II Continuous

I	will have been	being
you	will have been	being
he/she/it	will have been	being
we	will have been	being
you	will have been	being
they	will have been	being

IMPERATIVE

be

GERUND

being

PAST PARTICIPLE

been

CONDITIONAL

Conditional II

I	would	be
you	would	be
he/she/it	would	be
we	would	be
you	would	be
they	would	be

Conditional Past

I	would have	been
you	would have	been
he/she/it	would have	been
we	would have	been
you	would have	been
they	would have	been

BECOME

tornar-se

+ *-ing* → ~~e~~ (ver p. 8)

SIMPLE

Present Simple

I	become
you	become
he/she/it	becomes
we	become
you	become
they	become

Past Simple

I	became
you	became
he/she/it	became
we	became
you	became
they	became

Present Perfect

I	have	become
you	have	become
he/she/it	has	become
we	have	become
you	have	become
they	have	become

Past Perfect

I	had	become
you	had	become
he/she/it	had	become
we	had	become
you	had	become
they	had	become

CONTINUOUS

Present Continuous

I	am	becoming
you	are	becoming
he/she/it	is	becoming
we	are	becoming
you	are	becoming
they	are	becoming

Past Continuous

I	was	becoming
you	were	becoming
he/she/it	was	becoming
we	were	becoming
you	were	becoming
they	were	becoming

Present Perfect Continuous

I	have been	becoming
you	have been	becoming
he/she/it	has been	becoming
we	have been	becoming
you	have been	becoming
they	have been	becoming

Past Perfect Continuous

I	had been	becoming
you	had been	becoming
he/she/it	had been	becoming
we	had been	becoming
you	had been	becoming
they	had been	becoming

FUTURE

Future I

I	will	become
you	will	become
he/she/it	will	become
we	will	become
you	will	become
they	will	become

Future I Continuous

I	will be becoming
you	will be becoming
he/she/it	will be becoming
we	will be becoming
you	will be becoming
they	will be becoming

Future II

I	will have	become
you	will have	become
he/she/it	will have	become
we	will have	become
you	will have	become
they	will have	become

Future II Continuous

I	will have been	becoming
you	will have been	becoming
he/she/it	will have been	becoming
we	will have been	becoming
you	will have been	becoming
they	will have been	becoming

IMPERATIVE

become

GERUND

becoming

PAST PARTICIPLE

become

CONDITIONAL

Conditional II

I	would	become
you	would	become
he/she/it	would	become
we	would	become
you	would	become
they	would	become

Conditional Past

I	would have	become
you	would have	become
he/she/it	would have	become
we	would have	become
you	would have	become
they	would have	become

BEGIN

começar

Duplicação de consoante (ver p. 7)

SIMPLE

Present Simple

I	begin
you	begin
he/she/it	begins
we	begin
you	begin
they	begin

Past Simple

I	began
you	began
he/she/it	began
we	began
you	began
they	began

Present Perfect

I	have	begun
you	have	begun
he/she/it	has	begun
we	have	begun
you	have	begun
they	have	begun

Past Perfect

I	had	begun
you	had	begun
he/she/it	had	begun
we	had	begun
you	had	begun
they	had	begun

CONTINUOUS

Present Continuous

I	am	beginning
you	are	beginning
he/she/it	is	beginning
we	are	beginning
you	are	beginning
they	are	beginning

Past Continuous

I	was	beginning
you	were	beginning
he/she/it	was	beginning
we	were	beginning
you	were	beginning
they	were	beginning

Present Perfect Continuous

I	have been	beginning
you	have been	beginning
he/she/it	has been	beginning
we	have been	beginning
you	have been	beginning
they	have been	beginning

Past Perfect Continuous

I	had been	beginning
you	had been	beginning
he/she/it	had been	beginning
we	had been	beginning
you	had been	beginning
they	had been	beginning

FUTURE

Future I

I	will	begin
you	will	begin
he/she/it	will	begin
we	will	begin
you	will	begin
they	will	begin

Future I Continuous

I	will be beginning
you	will be beginning
he/she/it	will be beginning
we	will be beginning
you	will be beginning
they	will be beginning

Future II

I	will have	begun
you	will have	begun
he/she/it	will have	begun
we	will have	begun
you	will have	begun
they	will have	begun

Future II Continuous

I	will have been	beginning
you	will have been	beginning
he/she/it	will have been	beginning
we	will have been	beginning
you	will have been	beginning
they	will have been	beginning

IMPERATIVE

begin

GERUND

beginning

PAST PARTICIPLE

begun

CONDITIONAL

Conditional II

I	would	begin
you	would	begin
he/she/it	would	begin
we	would	begin
you	would	begin
they	would	begin

Conditional Past

I	would have	begun
you	would have	begun
he/she/it	would have	begun
we	would have	begun
you	would have	begun
they	would have	begun

BOOK
inscrever

SIMPLE

Present Simple

I	book
you	book
he/she/it	books
we	book
you	book
they	book

Past Simple

I	booked
you	booked
he/she/it	booked
we	booked
you	booked
they	booked

Present Perfect

I	have	booked
you	have	booked
he/she/it	has	booked
we	have	booked
you	have	booked
they	have	booked

Past Perfect

I	had	booked
you	had	booked
he/she/it	had	booked
we	had	booked
you	had	booked
they	had	booked

CONTINUOUS

Present Continuous

I	am	booking
you	are	booking
he/she/it	is	booking
we	are	booking
you	are	booking
they	are	booking

Past Continuous

I	was	booking
you	were	booking
he/she/it	was	booking
we	were	booking
you	were	booking
they	were	booking

Present Perfect Continuous

I	have been	booking
you	have been	booking
he/she/it	has been	booking
we	have been	booking
you	have been	booking
they	have been	booking

Past Perfect Continuous

I	had	been	booking
you	had	been	booking
he/she/it	had	been	booking
we	had	been	booking
you	had	been	booking
they	had	been	booking

FUTURE

Future I

I	will	book
you	will	book
he/she/it	will	book
we	will	book
you	will	book
they	will	book

Future I Continuous

I	will be booking
you	will be booking
he/she/it	will be booking
we	will be booking
you	will be booking
they	will be booking

Future II

I	will have	booked
you	will have	booked
he/she/it	will have	booked
we	will have	booked
you	will have	booked
they	will have	booked

Future II Continuous

I	will have been	booking
you	will have been	booking
he/she/it	will have been	booking
we	will have been	booking
you	will have been	booking
they	will have been	booking

IMPERATIVE
book

GERUND
booking

PAST PARTICIPLE
booked

CONDITIONAL

Conditional II

I	would	book
you	would	book
he/she/it	would	book
we	would	book
you	would	book
they	would	book

Conditional Past

I	would have	booked
you	would have	booked
he/she/it	would have	booked
we	would have	booked
you	would have	booked
they	would have	booked

BREAK
quebrar

SIMPLE

Present Simple

I	break
you	break
he/she/it	breaks
we	break
you	break
they	break

Past Simple

I	broke
you	broke
he/she/it	broke
we	broke
you	broke
they	broke

Present Perfect

I	have	broken
you	have	broken
he/she/it	has	broken
we	have	broken
you	have	broken
they	have	broken

Past Perfect

I	had	broken
you	had	broken
he/she/it	had	broken
we	had	broken
you	had	broken
they	had	broken

CONTINUOUS

Present Continuous

I	am	breaking
you	are	breaking
he/she/it	is	breaking
we	are	breaking
you	are	breaking
they	are	breaking

Past Continuous

I	was	breaking
you	were	breaking
he/she/it	was	breaking
we	were	breaking
you	were	breaking
they	were	breaking

Present Perfect Continuous

I	have been	breaking
you	have been	breaking
he/she/it	has been	breaking
we	have been	breaking
you	have been	breaking
they	have been	breaking

Past Perfect Continuous

I	had been	breaking
you	had been	breaking
he/she/it	had been	breaking
we	had been	breaking
you	had been	breaking
they	had been	breaking

FUTURE

Future I

I	will	break
you	will	break
he/she/it	will	break
we	will	break
you	will	break
they	will	break

Future I Continuous

I	will be breaking
you	will be breaking
he/she/it	will be breaking
we	will be breaking
you	will be breaking
they	will be breaking

Future II

I	will have	broken
you	will have	broken
he/she/it	will have	broken
we	will have	broken
you	will have	broken
they	will have	broken

Future II Continuous

I	will have been	breaking
you	will have been	breaking
he/she/it	will have been	breaking
we	will have been	breaking
you	will have been	breaking
they	will have been	breaking

IMPERATIVE
break

GERUND
breaking

PAST PARTICIPLE
broken

CONDITIONAL

Conditional II

I	would	break
you	would	break
he/she/it	would	break
we	would	break
you	would	break
they	would	break

Conditional Past

I	would have	broken
you	would have	broken
he/she/it	would have	broken
we	would have	broken
you	would have	broken
they	would have	broken

IRREGULAR

BRING
trazer

SIMPLE

Present Simple

I	bring
you	bring
he/she/it	brings
we	bring
you	bring
they	bring

Past Simple

I	brought
you	brought
he/she/it	brought
we	brought
you	brought
they	brought

Present Perfect

I	have	brought
you	have	brought
he/she/it	has	brought
we	have	brought
you	have	brought
they	have	brought

Past Perfect

I	had	brought
you	had	brought
he/she/it	had	brought
we	had	brought
you	had	brought
they	had	brought

CONTINUOUS

Present Continuous

I	am	bringing
you	are	bringing
he/she/it	is	bringing
we	are	bringing
you	are	bringing
they	are	bringing

Past Continuous

I	was	bringing
you	were	bringing
he/she/it	was	bringing
we	were	bringing
you	were	bringing
they	were	bringing

Present Perfect Continuous

I	have been	bringing
you	have been	bringing
he/she/it	has been	bringing
we	have been	bringing
you	have been	bringing
they	have been	bringing

Past Perfect Continuous

I	had been	bringing
you	had been	bringing
he/she/it	had been	bringing
we	had been	bringing
you	had been	bringing
they	had been	bringing

FUTURE

Future I

I	will	bring
you	will	bring
he/she/it	will	bring
we	will	bring
you	will	bring
they	will	bring

Future I Continuous

I	will be bringing
you	will be bringing
he/she/it	will be bringing
we	will be bringing
you	will be bringing
they	will be bringing

Future II

I	will have	brought
you	will have	brought
he/she/it	will have	brought
we	will have	brought
you	will have	brought
they	will have	brought

Future II Continuous

I	will have been	bringing
you	will have been	bringing
he/she/it	will have been	bringing
we	will have been	bringing
you	will have been	bringing
they	will have been	bringing

IMPERATIVE
bring

GERUND
bringing

PAST PARTICIPLE
brought

CONDITIONAL

Conditional II

I	would	bring
you	would	bring
he/she/it	would	bring
we	would	bring
you	would	bring
they	would	bring

Conditional Past

I	would have	brought
you	would have	brought
he/she/it	would have	brought
we	would have	brought
you	would have	brought
they	would have	brought

BUY
comprar

SIMPLE

Present Simple

I	buy
you	buy
he/she/it	buys
we	buy
you	buy
they	buy

Past Simple

I	bought
you	bought
he/she/it	bought
we	bought
you	bought
they	bought

Present Perfect

I	have	bought
you	have	bought
he/she/it	has	bought
we	have	bought
you	have	bought
they	have	bought

Past Perfect

I	had	bought
you	had	bought
he/she/it	had	bought
we	had	bought
you	had	bought
they	had	bought

CONTINUOUS

Present Continuous

I	am	buying
you	are	buying
he/she/it	is	buying
we	are	buying
you	are	buying
they	are	buying

Past Continuous

I	was	buying
you	were	buying
he/she/it	was	buying
we	were	buying
you	were	buying
they	were	buying

Present Perfect Continuous

I	have been	buying
you	have been	buying
he/she/it	has been	buying
we	have been	buying
you	have been	buying
they	have been	buying

Past Perfect Continuous

I	had been	buying
you	had been	buying
he/she/it	had been	buying
we	had been	buying
you	had been	buying
they	had been	buying

FUTURE

Future I

I	will	buy
you	will	buy
he/she/it	will	buy
we	will	buy
you	will	buy
they	will	buy

Future I Continuous

I	will be buying
you	will be buying
he/she/it	will be buying
we	will be buying
you	will be buying
they	will be buying

Future II

I	will have	bought
you	will have	bought
he/she/it	will have	bought
we	will have	bought
you	will have	bought
they	will have	bought

Future II Continuous

I	will have been	buying
you	will have been	buying
he/she/it	will have been	buying
we	will have been	buying
you	will have been	buying
they	will have been	buying

IMPERATIVE
buy

GERUND
buying

PAST PARTICIPLE
bought

CONDITIONAL

Conditional II

I	would	buy
you	would	buy
he/she/it	would	buy
we	would	buy
you	would	buy
they	would	buy

Conditional Past

I	would have	bought
you	would have	bought
he/she/it	would have	bought
we	would have	bought
you	would have	bought
they	would have	bought

REGULAR

CALL
chamar, telefonar

SIMPLE

Present Simple

I	call
you	call
he/she/it	calls
we	call
you	call
they	call

Past Simple

I	called
you	called
he/she/it	called
we	called
you	called
they	called

Present Perfect

I	have	called
you	have	called
he/she/it	has	called
we	have	called
you	have	called
they	have	called

Past Perfect

I	had	called
you	had	called
he/she/it	had	called
we	had	called
you	had	called
they	had	called

CONTINUOUS

Present Continuous

I	am	calling
you	are	calling
he/she/it	is	calling
we	are	calling
you	are	calling
they	are	calling

Past Continuous

I	was	calling
you	were	calling
he/she/it	was	calling
we	were	calling
you	were	calling
they	were	calling

Present Perfect Continuous

I	have been	calling
you	have been	calling
he/she/it	has been	calling
we	have been	calling
you	have been	calling
they	have been	calling

Past Perfect Continuous

I	had been	calling
you	had been	calling
he/she/it	had been	calling
we	had been	calling
you	had been	calling
they	had been	calling

FUTURE

Future I

I	will	call
you	will	call
he/she/it	will	call
we	will	call
you	will	call
they	will	call

Future I Continuous

I	will be calling
you	will be calling
he/she/it	will be calling
we	will be calling
you	will be calling
they	will be calling

Future II

I	will have	called
you	will have	called
he/she/it	will have	called
we	will have	called
you	will have	called
they	will have	called

Future II Continuous

I	will have been	calling
you	will have been	calling
he/she/it	will have been	calling
we	will have been	calling
you	will have been	calling
they	will have been	calling

IMPERATIVE
call

GERUND
calling

PAST PARTICIPLE
called

CONDITIONAL

Conditional II

I	would	call
you	would	call
he/she/it	would	call
we	would	call
you	would	call
they	would	call

Conditional Past

I	would have	called
you	would have	called
he/she/it	would have	called
we	would have	called
you	would have	called
they	would have	called

CAN / BE ABLE TO

poder, ser capaz de

Verbo modal defectivo — *Can* só é conjugado no *Present Simple* e no *Past Simple* (*could*).
Can / could / be able to não têm forma contínua.

SIMPLE

Present Simple

I	can / am able to
you	can / are able to
he/she/it	can / is able to
we	can / are able to
you	can / are able to
they	can / are able to

Past Simple

I	could / was able to
you	could / were able to
he/she/it	could / was able to
we	could / were able to
you	could / were able to
they	could / were able to

Present Perfect

I	have been able to
you	have been able to
he/she/it	has been able to
we	have been able to
you	have been able to
they	have been able to

Past Perfect

I	had been able to
you	had been able to
he/she/it	had been able to
we	had been able to
you	had been able to
they	had been able to

CONTINUOUS

Present Continuous

—

Past Continuous

—

Present Perfect Continuous

Past Perfect Continuous

—

FUTURE

Future I

I	will be able to
you	will be able to
he/she/it	will be able to
we	will be able to
you	will be able to
they	will be able to

Future I Continuous

—

Future II

I	will have been able to
you	will have been able to
he/she/it	will have been able to
we	will have been able to
you	will have been able to
they	will have been able to

Future II Continuous

—

IMPERATIVE

be able to

GERUND

being able to

PAST PARTICIPLE

been able to

CONDITIONAL

Conditional II

I	would be able to
you	would be able to
he/she/it	would be able to
we	would be able to
you	would be able to
they	would be able to

Conditional Past

I	would have been able to
you	would have been able to
he/she/it	would have been able to
we	would have been able to
you	would have been able to
they	would have been able to

CANCEL
cancelar

No IA o **-l** não se duplica.

SIMPLE

Present Simple

I	cancel
you	cancel
he/she/it	cancels
we	cancel
you	cancel
they	cancel

Past Simple

I	cancelled
you	cancelled
he/she/it	cancelled
we	cancelled
you	cancelled
they	cancelled

Present Perfect

I	have	cancelled
you	have	cancelled
he/she/it	has	cancelled
we	have	cancelled
you	have	cancelled
they	have	cancelled

Past Perfect

I	had	cancelled
you	had	cancelled
he/she/it	had	cancelled
we	had	cancelled
you	had	cancelled
they	had	cancelled

CONTINUOUS

Present Continuous

I	am	cancelling
you	are	cancelling
he/she/it	is	cancelling
we	are	cancelling
you	are	cancelling
they	are	cancelling

Past Continuous

I	was	cancelling
you	were	cancelling
he/she/it	was	cancelling
we	were	cancelling
you	were	cancelling
they	were	cancelling

Present Perfect Continuous

I	have	been	cancelling
you	have	been	cancelling
he/she/it	has	been	cancelling
we	have	been	cancelling
you	have	been	cancelling
they	have	been	cancelling

Past Perfect Continuous

I	had	been	cancelling
you	had	been	cancelling
he/she/it	had	been	cancelling
we	had	been	cancelling
you	had	been	cancelling
they	had	been	cancelling

FUTURE

Future I

I	will	cancel
you	will	cancel
he/she/it	will	cancel
we	will	cancel
you	will	cancel
they	will	cancel

Future I Continuous

I	will be cancelling
you	will be cancelling
he/she/it	will be cancelling
we	will be cancelling
you	will be cancelling
they	will be cancelling

Future II

I	will have	cancelled
you	will have	cancelled
he/she/it	will have	cancelled
we	will have	cancelled
you	will have	cancelled
they	will have	cancelled

Future II Continuous

I	will have been	cancelling
you	will have been	cancelling
he/she/it	will have been	cancelling
we	will have been	cancelling
you	will have been	cancelling
they	will have been	cancelling

IMPERATIVE
cancel

GERUND
cancelling

PAST PARTICIPLE
cancelled

CONDITIONAL

Conditional II

I	would	cancel
you	would	cancel
he/she/it	would	cancel
we	would	cancel
you	would	cancel
they	would	cancel

Conditional Past

I	would have	cancelled
you	would have	cancelled
he/she/it	would have	cancelled
we	would have	cancelled
you	would have	cancelled
they	would have	cancelled

CARRY
carregar

-y* → *-ie antes de ***-s*** / ***-y* → *-i*** antes de ***-ed*** (ver p. 7)

SIMPLE

Present Simple

I	carry
you	carry
he/she/it	carries
we	carry
you	carry
they	carry

Past Simple

I	carried
you	carried
he/she/it	carried
we	carried
you	carried
they	carried

Present Perfect

I	have	carried
you	have	carried
he/she/it	has	carried
we	have	carried
you	have	carried
they	have	carried

Past Perfect

I	had	carried
you	had	carried
he/she/it	had	carried
we	had	carried
you	had	carried
they	had	carried

CONTINUOUS

Present Continuous

I	am	carrying
you	are	carrying
he/she/it	is	carrying
we	are	carrying
you	are	carrying
they	are	carrying

Past Continuous

I	was	carrying
you	were	carrying
he/she/it	was	carrying
we	were	carrying
you	were	carrying
they	were	carrying

Present Perfect Continuous

I	have been	carrying
you	have been	carrying
he/she/it	has been	carrying
we	have been	carrying
you	have been	carrying
they	have been	carrying

Past Perfect Continuous

I	had been	carrying
you	had been	carrying
he/she/it	had been	carrying
we	had been	carrying
you	had been	carrying
they	had been	carrying

FUTURE

Future I

I	will	carry
you	will	carry
he/she/it	will	carry
we	will	carry
you	will	carry
they	will	carry

Future I Continuous

I	will be carrying
you	will be carrying
he/she/it	will be carrying
we	will be carrying
you	will be carrying
they	will be carrying

Future II

I	will have carried
you	will have carried
he/she/it	will have carried
we	will have carried
you	will have carried
they	will have carried

Future II Continuous

I	will have been carrying
you	will have been carrying
he/she/it	will have been carrying
we	will have been carrying
you	will have been carrying
they	will have been carrying

IMPERATIVE
carry

GERUND
carrying

PAST PARTICIPLE
carried

CONDITIONAL

Conditional II

I	would	carry
you	would	carry
he/she/it	would	carry
we	would	carry
you	would	carry
they	would	carry

Conditional Past

I	would have	carried
you	would have	carried
he/she/it	would have	carried
we	would have	carried
you	would have	carried
they	would have	carried

IRREGULAR

CATCH
agarrar

+ **-es** na 3ª pessoa do singular do *Present Simple* (ver p. 7)

SIMPLE

Present Simple

I	catch
you	catch
he/she/it	catches
we	catch
you	catch
they	catch

Past Simple

I	caught
you	caught
he/she/it	caught
we	caught
you	caught
they	caught

Present Perfect

I	have	caught
you	have	caught
he/she/it	has	caught
we	have	caught
you	have	caught
they	have	caught

Past Perfect

I	had	caught
you	had	caught
he/she/it	had	caught
we	had	caught
you	had	caught
they	had	caught

CONTINUOUS

Present Continuous

I	am	catching
you	are	catching
he/she/it	is	catching
we	are	catching
you	are	catching
they	are	catching

Past Continuous

I	was	catching
you	were	catching
he/she/it	was	catching
we	were	catching
you	were	catching
they	were	catching

Present Perfect Continuous

I	have been	catching
you	have been	catching
he/she/it	has been	catching
we	have been	catching
you	have been	catching
they	have been	catching

Past Perfect Continuous

I	had been	catching
you	had been	catching
he/she/it	had been	catching
we	had been	catching
you	had been	catching
they	had been	catching

FUTURE

Future I

I	will	catch
you	will	catch
he/she/it	will	catch
we	will	catch
you	will	catch
they	will	catch

Future I Continuous

I	will be catching
you	will be catching
he/she/it	will be catching
we	will be catching
you	will be catching
they	will be catching

Future II

I	will have	caught
you	will have	caught
he/she/it	will have	caught
we	will have	caught
you	will have	caught
they	will have	caught

Future II Continuous

I	will have been	catching
you	will have been	catching
he/she/it	will have been	catching
we	will have been	catching
you	will have been	catching
they	will have been	catching

IMPERATIVE
catch

GERUND
catching

PAST PARTICIPLE
caught

CONDITIONAL

Conditional II

I	would	catch
you	would	catch
he/she/it	would	catch
we	would	catch
you	would	catch
they	would	catch

Conditional Past

I	would have	caught
you	would have	caught
he/she/it	would have	caught
we	would have	caught
you	would have	caught
they	would have	caught

CHANGE

mudar, trocar

+ *-ing* → ~~e~~ (ver p. 8) / + *-d* não *-ed* (ver p. 7)

SIMPLE

Present Simple

I	change
you	change
he/she/it	change**s**
we	change
you	change
they	change

Past Simple

I	changed
you	changed
he/she/it	changed
we	changed
you	changed
they	changed

Present Perfect

I	have	changed
you	have	changed
he/she/it	has	changed
we	have	changed
you	have	changed
they	have	changed

Past Perfect

I	had	changed
you	had	changed
he/she/it	had	changed
we	had	changed
you	had	changed
they	had	changed

CONTINUOUS

Present Continuous

I	am	changing
you	are	changing
he/she/it	is	changing
we	are	changing
you	are	changing
they	are	changing

Past Continuous

I	was	changing
you	were	changing
he/she/it	was	changing
we	were	changing
you	were	changing
they	were	changing

Present Perfect Continuous

I	have been	changing
you	have been	changing
he/she/it	has been	changing
we	have been	changing
you	have been	changing
they	have been	changing

Past Perfect Continuous

I	had been	changing
you	had been	changing
he/she/it	had been	changing
we	had been	changing
you	had been	changing
they	had been	changing

FUTURE

Future I

I	will	change
you	will	change
he/she/it	will	change
we	will	change
you	will	change
they	will	change

Future I Continuous

I	will be changing
you	will be changing
he/she/it	will be changing
we	will be changing
you	will be changing
they	will be changing

Future II

I	will have	changed
you	will have	changed
he/she/it	will have	changed
we	will have	changed
you	will have	changed
they	will have	changed

Future II Continuous

I	will have been	changing
you	will have been	changing
he/she/it	will have been	changing
we	will have been	changing
you	will have been	changing
they	will have been	changing

IMPERATIVE

change

GERUND

changing

PAST PARTICIPLE

changed

CONDITIONAL

Conditional II

I	would	change
you	would	change
he/she/it	would	change
we	would	change
you	would	change
they	would	change

Conditional Past

I	would have	changed
you	would have	changed
he/she/it	would have	changed
we	would have	changed
you	would have	changed
they	would have	changed

IRREGULAR

CHOOSE

escolher

+ *-ing* → ~~e~~ (ver p. 8)

SIMPLE

Present Simple

I	choose
you	choose
he/she/it	chooses
we	choose
you	choose
they	choose

Past Simple

I	chose
you	chose
he/she/it	chose
we	chose
you	chose
they	chose

Present Perfect

I	have	chosen
you	have	chosen
he/she/it	has	chosen
we	have	chosen
you	have	chosen
they	have	chosen

Past Perfect

I	had	chosen
you	had	chosen
he/she/it	had	chosen
we	had	chosen
you	had	chosen
they	had	chosen

CONTINUOUS

Present Continuous

I	am	choosing
you	are	choosing
he/she/it	is	choosing
we	are	choosing
you	are	choosing
they	are	choosing

Past Continuous

I	was	choosing
you	were	choosing
he/she/it	was	choosing
we	were	choosing
you	were	choosing
they	were	choosing

Present Perfect Continuous

I	have been	choosing
you	have been	choosing
he/she/it	has been	choosing
we	have been	choosing
you	have been	choosing
they	have been	choosing

Past Perfect Continuous

I	had been	choosing
you	had been	choosing
he/she/it	had been	choosing
we	had been	choosing
you	had been	choosing
they	had been	choosing

FUTURE

Future I

I	will	choose
you	will	choose
he/she/it	will	choose
we	will	choose
you	will	choose
they	will	choose

Future I Continuous

I	will be choosing
you	will be choosing
he/she/it	will be choosing
we	will be choosing
you	will be choosing
they	will be choosing

Future II

I	will have	chosen
you	will have	chosen
he/she/it	will have	chosen
we	will have	chosen
you	will have	chosen
they	will have	chosen

Future II Continuous

I	will have been	choosing
you	will have been	choosing
he/she/it	will have been	choosing
we	will have been	choosing
you	will have been	choosing
they	will have been	choosing

IMPERATIVE

choose

GERUND

choosing

PAST PARTICIPLE

chosen

CONDITIONAL

Conditional II

I	would	choose
you	would	choose
he/she/it	would	choose
we	would	choose
you	would	choose
they	would	choose

Conditional Past

I	would have	chosen
you	would have	chosen
he/she/it	would have	chosen
we	would have	chosen
you	would have	chosen
they	would have	chosen

CLOSE

fechar

+ ***-ing*** → e̸ (ver p. 8) / + ***-d*** não ***-ed*** (ver p. 7)

SIMPLE

Present Simple

I	close
you	close
he/she/it	closes
we	close
you	close
they	close

Past Simple

I	closed
you	closed
he/she/it	closed
we	closed
you	closed
they	closed

Present Perfect

I	have	closed
you	have	closed
he/she/it	has	closed
we	have	closed
you	have	closed
they	have	closed

Past Perfect

I	had	closed
you	had	closed
he/she/it	had	closed
we	had	closed
you	had	closed
they	had	closed

CONTINUOUS

Present Continuous

I	am	closing
you	are	closing
he/she/it	is	closing
we	are	closing
you	are	closing
they	are	closing

Past Continuous

I	was	closing
you	were	closing
he/she/it	was	closing
we	were	closing
you	were	closing
they	were	closing

Present Perfect Continuous

I	have been	closing
you	have been	closing
he/she/it	has been	closing
we	have been	closing
you	have been	closing
they	have been	closing

Past Perfect Continuous

I	had	been	closing
you	had	been	closing
he/she/it	had	been	closing
we	had	been	closing
you	had	been	closing
they	had	been	closing

FUTURE

Future I

I	will	close
you	will	close
he/she/it	will	close
we	will	close
you	will	close
they	will	close

Future I Continuous

I	will be closing
you	will be closing
he/she/it	will be closing
we	will be closing
you	will be closing
they	will be closing

Future II

I	will have	closed
you	will have	closed
he/she/it	will have	closed
we	will have	closed
you	will have	closed
they	will have	closed

Future II Continuous

I	will have been	closing
you	will have been	closing
he/she/it	will have been	closing
we	will have been	closing
you	will have been	closing
they	will have been	closing

IMPERATIVE

close

GERUND

closing

PAST PARTICIPLE

closed

CONDITIONAL

Conditional II

I	would	close
you	would	close
he/she/it	would	close
we	would	close
you	would	close
they	would	close

Conditional Past

I	would have	closed
you	would have	closed
he/she/it	would have	closed
we	would have	closed
you	would have	closed
they	would have	closed

COME
vir

+ ***-ing*** → ~~e~~ (ver p. 8)

SIMPLE

Present Simple

I	come
you	come
he/she/it	comes
we	come
you	come
they	come

Past Simple

I	**came**
you	**came**
he/she/it	**came**
we	**came**
you	**came**
they	**came**

Present Perfect

I	have	come
you	have	come
he/she/it	has	come
we	have	come
you	have	come
they	have	come

Past Perfect

I	had	come
you	had	come
he/she/it	had	come
we	had	come
you	had	come
they	had	come

CONTINUOUS

Present Continuous

I	am	coming
you	are	coming
he/she/it	is	coming
we	are	coming
you	are	coming
they	are	coming

Past Continuous

I	was	coming
you	were	coming
he/she/it	was	coming
we	were	coming
you	were	coming
they	were	coming

Present Perfect Continuous

I	have been	coming
you	have been	coming
he/she/it	has been	coming
we	have been	coming
you	have been	coming
they	have been	coming

Past Perfect Continuous

I	had been	coming
you	had been	coming
he/she/it	had been	coming
we	had been	coming
you	had been	coming
they	had been	coming

FUTURE

Future I

I	will	come
you	will	come
he/she/it	will	come
we	will	come
you	will	come
they	will	come

Future I Continuous

I	will be coming
you	will be coming
he/she/it	will be coming
we	will be coming
you	will be coming
they	will be coming

Future II

I	will have come
you	will have come
he/she/it	will have come
we	will have come
you	will have come
they	will have come

Future II Continuous

I	will have been	coming
you	will have been	coming
he/she/it	will have been	coming
we	will have been	coming
you	will have been	coming
they	will have been	coming

IMPERATIVE
come

GERUND
coming

PAST PARTICIPLE
come

CONDITIONAL

Conditional II

I	would	come
you	would	come
he/she/it	would	come
we	would	come
you	would	come
they	would	come

Conditional Past

I	would have	come
you	would have	come
he/she/it	would have	come
we	would have	come
you	would have	come
they	would have	come

COOK
cozinhar

SIMPLE

Present Simple

I	cook
you	cook
he/she/it	cooks
we	cook
you	cook
they	cook

Past Simple

I	cooked
you	cooked
he/she/it	cooked
we	cooked
you	cooked
they	cooked

Present Perfect

I	have	cooked
you	have	cooked
he/she/it	has	cooked
we	have	cooked
you	have	cooked
they	have	cooked

Past Perfect

I	had	cooked
you	had	cooked
he/she/it	had	cooked
we	had	cooked
you	had	cooked
they	had	cooked

CONTINUOUS

Present Continuous

I	am	cooking
you	are	cooking
he/she/it	is	cooking
we	are	cooking
you	are	cooking
they	are	cooking

Past Continuous

I	was	cooking
you	were	cooking
he/she/it	was	cooking
we	were	cooking
you	were	cooking
they	were	cooking

Present Perfect Continuous

I	have been	cooking
you	have been	cooking
he/she/it	has been	cooking
we	have been	cooking
you	have been	cooking
they	have been	cooking

Past Perfect Continuous

I	had been	cooking
you	had been	cooking
he/she/it	had been	cooking
we	had been	cooking
you	had been	cooking
they	had been	cooking

FUTURE

Future I

I	will	cook
you	will	cook
he/she/it	will	cook
we	will	cook
you	will	cook
they	will	cook

Future I Continuous

I	will be cooking
you	will be cooking
he/she/it	will be cooking
we	will be cooking
you	will be cooking
they	will be cooking

Future II

I	will have	cooked
you	will have	cooked
he/she/it	will have	cooked
we	will have	cooked
you	will have	cooked
they	will have	cooked

Future II Continuous

I	will have been	cooking
you	will have been	cooking
he/she/it	will have been	cooking
we	will have been	cooking
you	will have been	cooking
they	will have been	cooking

IMPERATIVE
cook

GERUND
cooking

PAST PARTICIPLE
cooked

CONDITIONAL

Conditional II

I	would	cook
you	would	cook
he/she/it	would	cook
we	would	cook
you	would	cook
they	would	cook

Conditional Past

I	would have	cooked
you	would have	cooked
he/she/it	would have	cooked
we	would have	cooked
you	would have	cooked
they	would have	cooked

IRREGULAR

COST
custar

SIMPLE

Present Simple

I	cost
you	cost
he/she/it	costs
we	cost
you	cost
they	cost

Past Simple

I	cost
you	cost
he/she/it	cost
we	cost
you	cost
they	cost

Present Perfect

I	have	cost
you	have	cost
he/she/it	has	cost
we	have	cost
you	have	cost
they	have	cost

Past Perfect

I	had	cost
you	had	cost
he/she/it	had	cost
we	had	cost
you	had	cost
they	had	cost

CONTINUOUS

Present Continuous

I	am	costing
you	are	costing
he/she/it	is	costing
we	are	costing
you	are	costing
they	are	costing

Past Continuous

I	was	costing
you	were	costing
he/she/it	was	costing
we	were	costing
you	were	costing
they	were	costing

Present Perfect Continuous

I	have been	costing
you	have been	costing
he/she/it	has been	costing
we	have been	costing
you	have been	costing
they	have been	costing

Past Perfect Continuous

I	had been	costing
you	had been	costing
he/she/it	had been	costing
we	had been	costing
you	had been	costing
they	had been	costing

FUTURE

Future I

I	will	cost
you	will	cost
he/she/it	will	cost
we	will	cost
you	will	cost
they	will	cost

Future I Continuous

I	will be costing
you	will be costing
he/she/it	will be costing
we	will be costing
you	will be costing
they	will be costing

Future II

I	will have cost
you	will have cost
he/she/it	will have cost
we	will have cost
you	will have cost
they	will have cost

Future II Continuous

I	will have been	costing
you	will have been	costing
he/she/it	will have been	costing
we	will have been	costing
you	will have been	costing
they	will have been	costing

IMPERATIVE
cost

GERUND
costing

PAST PARTICIPLE
cost

CONDITIONAL

Conditional II

I	would	cost
you	would	cost
he/she/it	would	cost
we	would	cost
you	would	cost
they	would	cost

Conditional Past

I	would have	cost
you	would have	cost
he/she/it	would have	cost
we	would have	cost
you	would have	cost
they	would have	cost

CUT
cortar

Duplicação da consoante (ver p. 7)

SIMPLE

Present Simple

I	cut
you	cut
he/she/it	cuts
we	cut
you	cut
they	cut

Past Simple

I	cut
you	cut
he/she/it	cut
we	cut
you	cut
they	cut

Present Perfect

I	have cut
you	have cut
he/she/it	has cut
we	have cut
you	have cut
they	have cut

Past Perfect

I	had cut
you	had cut
he/she/it	had cut
we	had cut
you	had cut
they	had cut

CONTINUOUS

Present Continuous

I	am cutting
you	are cutting
he/she/it	is cutting
we	are cutting
you	are cutting
they	are cutting

Past Continuous

I	was cutting
you	were cutting
he/she/it	was cutting
we	were cutting
you	were cutting
they	were cutting

Present Perfect Continuous

I	have been cutting
you	have been cutting
he/she/it	has been cutting
we	have been cutting
you	have been cutting
they	have been cutting

Past Perfect Continuous

I	had been cutting
you	had been cutting
he/she/it	had been cutting
we	had been cutting
you	had been cutting
they	had been cutting

FUTURE

Future I

I	will cut
you	will cut
he/she/it	will cut
we	will cut
you	will cut
they	will cut

Future I Continuous

I	will be cutting
you	will be cutting
he/she/it	will be cutting
we	will be cutting
you	will be cutting
they	will be cutting

Future II

I	will have cut
you	will have cut
he/she/it	will have cut
we	will have cut
you	will have cut
they	will have cut

Future II Continuous

I	will have been cutting
you	will have been cutting
he/she/it	will have been cutting
we	will have been cutting
you	will have been cutting
they	will have been cutting

IMPERATIVE
cut

GERUND
cutting

PAST PARTICIPLE
cut

CONDITIONAL

Conditional II

I	would cut
you	would cut
he/she/it	would cut
we	would cut
you	would cut
they	would cut

Conditional Past

I	would have cut
you	would have cut
he/she/it	would have cut
we	would have cut
you	would have cut
they	would have cut

REGULAR

DECIDE
decidir

+ *-ing* → ~~e~~ (ver p. 8) / + *-d* não *-ed* (ver p. 7)

SIMPLE

Present Simple

I	decide
you	decide
he/she/it	decides
we	decide
you	decide
they	decide

Past Simple

I	decided
you	decided
he/she/it	decided
we	decided
you	decided
they	decided

Present Perfect

I	have	decided
you	have	decided
he/she/it	has	decided
we	have	decided
you	have	decided
they	have	decided

Past Perfect

I	had	decided
you	had	decided
he/she/it	had	decided
we	had	decided
you	had	decided
they	had	decided

CONTINUOUS

Present Continuous

I	am	deciding
you	are	deciding
he/she/it	is	deciding
we	are	deciding
you	are	deciding
they	are	deciding

Past Continuous

I	was	deciding
you	were	deciding
he/she/it	was	deciding
we	were	deciding
you	were	deciding
they	were	deciding

Present Perfect Continuous

I	have been	deciding
you	have been	deciding
he/she/it	has been	deciding
we	have been	deciding
you	have been	deciding
they	have been	deciding

Past Perfect Continuous

I	had been	deciding
you	had been	deciding
he/she/it	had been	deciding
we	had been	deciding
you	had been	deciding
they	had been	deciding

FUTURE

Future I

I	will	decide
you	will	decide
he/she/it	will	decide
we	will	decide
you	will	decide
they	will	decide

Future I Continuous

I	will be deciding
you	will be deciding
he/she/it	will be deciding
we	will be deciding
you	will be deciding
they	will be deciding

Future II

I	will have	decided
you	will have	decided
he/she/it	will have	decided
we	will have	decided
you	will have	decided
they	will have	decided

Future II Continuous

I	will have been	deciding
you	will have been	deciding
he/she/it	will have been	deciding
we	will have been	deciding
you	will have been	deciding
they	will have been	deciding

IMPERATIVE
decide

GERUND
deciding

PAST PARTICIPLE
decided

CONDITIONAL

Conditional II

I	would	decide
you	would	decide
he/she/it	would	decide
we	would	decide
you	would	decide
they	would	decide

Conditional Past

I	would have	decided
you	would have	decided
he/she/it	would have	decided
we	would have	decided
you	would have	decided
they	would have	decided

DO
fazer

+ -***es*** na 3ª pessoa do singular do *Present Simple* (ver p. 7)

SIMPLE

Present Simple

I	do
you	do
he/she/it	**does**
we	do
you	do
they	do

Past Simple

I	**did**
you	**did**
he/she/it	**did**
we	**did**
you	**did**
they	**did**

Present Perfect

I	have	**done**
you	have	**done**
he/she/it	has	**done**
we	have	**done**
you	have	**done**
they	have	**done**

Past Perfect

I	had	**done**
you	had	**done**
he/she/it	had	**done**
we	had	**done**
you	had	**done**
they	had	**done**

CONTINUOUS

Present Continuous

I	am	doing
you	are	doing
he/she/it	is	doing
we	are	doing
you	are	doing
they	are	doing

Past Continuous

I	was	doing
you	were	doing
he/she/it	was	doing
we	were	doing
you	were	doing
they	were	doing

Present Perfect Continuous

I	have been	doing
you	have been	doing
he/she/it	has been	doing
we	have been	doing
you	have been	doing
they	have been	doing

Past Perfect Continuous

I	had been	doing
you	had been	doing
he/she/it	had been	doing
we	had been	doing
you	had been	doing
they	had been	doing

FUTURE

Future I

I	will	do
you	will	do
he/she/it	will	do
we	will	do
you	will	do
they	will	do

Future I Continuous

I	will be doing
you	will be doing
he/she/it	will be doing
we	will be doing
you	will be doing
they	will be doing

Future II

I	will have	**done**
you	will have	**done**
he/she/it	will have	**done**
we	will have	**done**
you	will have	**done**
they	will have	**done**

Future II Continuous

I	will have been	doing
you	will have been	doing
he/she/it	will have been	doing
we	will have been	doing
you	will have been	doing
they	will have been	doing

IMPERATIVE
do

GERUND
doing

PAST PARTICIPLE
done

CONDITIONAL

Conditional II

I	would	do
you	would	do
he/she/it	would	do
we	would	do
you	would	do
they	would	do

Conditional Past

I	would have	**done**
you	would have	**done**
he/she/it	would have	**done**
wedo	would have	**done**
you	would have	**done**
they	would have	**done**

DRINK
beber

SIMPLE

Present Simple

I	drink
you	drink
he/she/it	drinks
we	drink
you	drink
they	drink

Past Simple

I	drank
you	drank
he/she/it	drank
we	drank
you	drank
they	drank

Present Perfect

I	have	drunk
you	have	drunk
he/she/it	has	drunk
we	have	drunk
you	have	drunk
they	have	drunk

Past Perfect

I	had	drunk
you	had	drunk
he/she/it	had	drunk
we	had	drunk
you	had	drunk
they	had	drunk

CONTINUOUS

Present Continuous

I	am	drinking
you	are	drinking
he/she/it	is	drinking
we	are	drinking
you	are	drinking
they	are	drinking

Past Continuous

I	was	drinking
you	were	drinking
he/she/it	was	drinking
we	were	drinking
you	were	drinking
they	were	drinking

Present Perfect Continuous

I	have been	drinking
you	have been	drinking
he/she/it	has been	drinking
we	have been	drinking
you	have been	drinking
they	have been	drinking

Past Perfect Continuous

I	had been	drinking
you	had been	drinking
he/she/it	had been	drinking
we	had been	drinking
you	had been	drinking
they	had been	drinking

FUTURE

Future I

I	will	drink
you	will	drink
he/she/it	will	drink
we	will	drink
you	will	drink
they	will	drink

Future I Continuous

I	will be drinking
you	will be drinking
he/she/it	will be drinking
we	will be drinking
you	will be drinking
they	will be drinking

Future II

I	will have drunk
you	will have drunk
he/she/it	will have drunk
we	will have drunk
you	will have drunk
they	will have drunk

Future II Continuous

I	will have been	drinking
you	will have been	drinking
he/she/it	will have been	drinking
we	will have been	drinking
you	will have been	drinking
they	will have been	drinking

IMPERATIVE
drink

GERUND
drinking

PAST PARTICIPLE
drunk

CONDITIONAL

Conditional II

I	would	drink
you	would	drink
he/she/it	would	drink
we	would	drink
you	would	drink
they	would	drink

Conditional Past

I	would have	drunk
you	would have	drunk
he/she/it	would have	drunk
we	would have	drunk
you	would have	drunk
they	would have	drunk

DRIVE
dirigir

+ *-ing* → ~~e~~ (ver p. 8)

SIMPLE

Present Simple

I	drive
you	drive
he/she/it	drives
we	drive
you	drive
they	drive

Past Simple

I	drove
you	drove
he/she/it	drove
we	drove
you	drove
they	drove

Present Perfect

I	have	driven
you	have	driven
he/she/it	has	driven
we	have	driven
you	have	driven
they	have	driven

Past Perfect

I	had	driven
you	had	driven
he/she/it	had	driven
we	had	driven
you	had	driven
they	had	driven

CONTINUOUS

Present Continuous

I	am	driving
you	are	driving
he/she/it	is	driving
we	are	driving
you	are	driving
they	are	driving

Past Continuous

I	was	driving
you	were	driving
he/she/it	was	driving
we	were	driving
you	were	driving
they	were	driving

Present Perfect Continuous

I	have been	driving
you	have been	driving
he/she/it	has been	driving
we	have been	driving
you	have been	driving
they	have been	driving

Past Perfect Continuous

I	had been	driving
you	had been	driving
he/she/it	had been	driving
we	had been	driving
you	had been	driving
they	had been	driving

FUTURE

Future I

I	will	drive
you	will	drive
he/she/it	will	drive
we	will	drive
you	will	drive
they	will	drive

Future I Continuous

I	will be driving
you	will be driving
he/she/it	will be driving
we	will be driving
you	will be driving
they	will be driving

Future II

I	will have	driven
you	will have	driven
he/she/it	will have	driven
we	will have	driven
you	will have	driven
they	will have	driven

Future II Continuous

I	will have been	driving
you	will have been	driving
he/she/it	will have been	driving
we	will have been	driving
you	will have been	driving
they	will have been	driving

IMPERATIVE
drive

GERUND
driving

PAST PARTICIPLE
driven

CONDITIONAL

Conditional II

I	would	drive
you	would	drive
he/she/it	would	drive
we	would	drive
you	would	drive
they	would	drive

Conditional Past

I	would have	driven
you	would have	driven
he/she/it	would have	driven
we	would have	driven
you	would have	driven
they	would have	driven

EAT
comer

SIMPLE

Present Simple

I	eat
you	eat
he/she/it	eats
we	eat
you	eat
they	eat

Past Simple

I	**ate**
you	**ate**
he/she/it	**ate**
we	**ate**
you	**ate**
they	**ate**

Present Perfect

I	have	**eaten**
you	have	**eaten**
he/she/it	has	**eaten**
we	have	**eaten**
you	have	**eaten**
they	have	**eaten**

Past Perfect

I	had	**eaten**
you	had	**eaten**
he/she/it	had	**eaten**
we	had	**eaten**
you	had	**eaten**
they	had	**eaten**

CONTINUOUS

Present Continuous

I	am	eating
you	are	eating
he/she/it	is	eating
we	are	eating
you	are	eating
they	are	eating

Past Continuous

I	was	eating
you	were	eating
he/she/it	was	eating
we	were	eating
you	were	eating
they	were	eating

Present Perfect Continuous

I	have been	eating
you	have been	eating
he/she/it	has been	eating
we	have been	eating
you	have been	eating
they	have been	eating

Past Perfect Continuous

I	had been	eating
you	had been	eating
he/she/it	had been	eating
we	had been	eating
you	had been	eating
they	had been	eating

FUTURE

Future I

I	will	eat
you	will	eat
he/she/it	will	eat
we	will	eat
you	will	eat
they	will	eat

Future I Continuous

I	will be eating
you	will be eating
he/she/it	will be eating
we	will be eating
you	will be eating
they	will be eating

Future II

I	will have	**eaten**
you	will have	**eaten**
he/she/it	will have	**eaten**
we	will have	**eaten**
you	will have	**eaten**
they	will have	**eaten**

Future II Continuous

I	will have been	eating
you	will have been	eating
he/she/it	will have been	eating
we	will have been	eating
you	will have been	eating
they	will have been	eating

IMPERATIVE
eat

GERUND
eating

PAST PARTICIPLE
eaten

CONDITIONAL

Conditional II

I	would	eat
you	would	eat
he/she/it	would	eat
we	would	eat
you	would	eat
they	would	eat

Conditional Past

I	would have	**eaten**
you	would have	**eaten**
he/she/it	would have	**eaten**
we	would have	**eaten**
you	would have	**eaten**
they	would have	**eaten**

ENJOY
desfrutar

SIMPLE

Present Simple

I	enjoy
you	enjoy
he/she/it	enjoys
we	enjoy
you	enjoy
they	enjoy

Past Simple

I	enjoyed
you	enjoyed
he/she/it	enjoyed
we	enjoyed
you	enjoyed
they	enjoyed

Present Perfect

I	have	enjoyed
you	have	enjoyed
he/she/it	has	enjoyed
we	have	enjoyed
you	have	enjoyed
they	have	enjoyed

Past Perfect

I	had	enjoyed
you	had	enjoyed
he/she/it	had	enjoyed
we	had	enjoyed
you	had	enjoyed
they	had	enjoyed

CONTINUOUS

Present Continuous

I	am	enjoying
you	are	enjoying
he/she/it	is	enjoying
we	are	enjoying
you	are	enjoying
they	are	enjoying

Past Continuous

I	was	enjoying
you	were	enjoying
he/she/it	was	enjoying
we	were	enjoying
you	were	enjoying
they	were	enjoying

Present Perfect Continuous

I	have	been	enjoying
you	have	been	enjoying
he/she/it	has	been	enjoying
we	have	been	enjoying
you	have	been	enjoying
they	have	been	enjoying

Past Perfect Continuous

I	had	been	enjoying
you	had	been	enjoying
he/she/it	had	been	enjoying
we	had	been	enjoying
you	had	been	enjoying
they	had	been	enjoying

FUTURE

Future I

I	will	enjoy
you	will	enjoy
he/she/it	will	enjoy
we	will	enjoy
you	will	enjoy
they	will	enjoy

Future I Continuous

I	will be enjoying
you	will be enjoying
he/she/it	will be enjoying
we	will be enjoying
you	will be enjoying
they	will be enjoying

Future II

I	will have	enjoyed
you	will have	enjoyed
he/she/it	will have	enjoyed
we	will have	enjoyed
you	will have	enjoyed
they	will have	enjoyed

Future II Continuous

I	will have been	enjoying
you	will have been	enjoying
he/she/it	will have been	enjoying
we	will have been	enjoying
you	will have been	enjoying
they	will have been	enjoying

IMPERATIVE
enjoy

GERUND
enjoying

PAST PARTICIPLE
enjoyed

CONDITIONAL

Conditional II

I	would	enjoy
you	would	enjoy
he/she/it	would	enjoy
we	would	enjoy
you	would	enjoy
they	would	enjoy

Conditional Past

I	would have	enjoyed
you	would have	enjoyed
he/she/it	would have	enjoyed
we	would have	enjoyed
you	would have	enjoyed
they	would have	enjoyed

FALL
cair

SIMPLE

Present Simple

I	fall
you	fall
he/she/it	falls
we	fall
you	fall
they	fall

Past Simple

I	fell
you	fell
he/she/it	fell
we	fell
you	fell
they	fell

Present Perfect

I	have	fallen
you	have	fallen
he/she/it	has	fallen
we	have	fallen
you	have	fallen
they	have	fallen

Past Perfect

I	had	fallen
you	had	fallen
he/she/it	had	fallen
we	had	fallen
you	had	fallen
they	had	fallen

CONTINUOUS

Present Continuous

I	am	falling
you	are	falling
he/she/it	is	falling
we	are	falling
you	are	falling
they	are	falling

Past Continuous

I	was	falling
you	were	falling
he/she/it	was	falling
we	were	falling
you	were	falling
they	were	falling

Present Perfect Continuous

I	have been	falling
you	have been	falling
he/she/it	has been	falling
we	have been	falling
you	have been	falling
they	have been	falling

Past Perfect Continuous

I	had been	falling
you	had been	falling
he/she/it	had been	falling
we	had been	falling
you	had been	falling
they	had been	falling

FUTURE

Future I

I	will	fall
you	will	fall
he/she/it	will	fall
we	will	fall
you	will	fall
they	will	fall

Future I Continuous

I	will be falling
you	will be falling
he/she/it	will be falling
we	will be falling
you	will be falling
they	will be falling

Future II

I	will have	fallen
you	will have	fallen
he/she/it	will have	fallen
we	will have	fallen
you	will have	fallen
they	will have	fallen

Future II Continuous

I	will have been	falling
you	will have been	falling
he/she/it	will have been	falling
we	will have been	falling
you	will have been	falling
they	will have been	falling

IMPERATIVE
fall

GERUND
falling

PAST PARTICIPLE
fallen

CONDITIONAL

Conditional II

I	would	fall
you	would	fall
he/she/it	would	fall
we	would	fall
you	would	fall
they	would	fall

Conditional Past

I	would have	fallen
you	would have	fallen
he/she/it	would have	fallen
we	would have	fallen
you	would have	fallen
they	would have	fallen

FEEL
sentir

SIMPLE

Present Simple

I	feel
you	feel
he/she/it	feels
we	feel
you	feel
they	feel

Past Simple

I	felt
you	felt
he/she/it	felt
we	felt
you	felt
they	felt

Present Perfect

I	have	felt
you	have	felt
he/she/it	has	felt
we	have	felt
you	have	felt
they	have	felt

Past Perfect

I	had	felt
you	had	felt
he/she/it	had	felt
we	had	felt
you	had	felt
they	had	felt

CONTINUOUS

Present Continuous

I	am	feeling
you	are	feeling
he/she/it	is	feeling
we	are	feeling
you	are	feeling
they	are	feeling

Past Continuous

I	was	feeling
you	were	feeling
he/she/it	was	feeling
we	were	feeling
you	were	feeling
they	were	feeling

Present Perfect Continuous

I	have been	feeling
you	have been	feeling
he/she/it	has been	feeling
we	have been	feeling
you	have been	feeling
they	have been	feeling

Past Perfect Continuous

I	had been	feeling
you	had been	feeling
he/she/it	had been	feeling
we	had been	feeling
you	had been	feeling
they	had been	feeling

FUTURE

Future I

I	will	feel
you	will	feel
he/she/it	will	feel
we	will	feel
you	will	feel
they	will	feel

Future I Continuous

I	will be feeling
you	will be feeling
he/she/it	will be feeling
we	will be feeling
you	will be feeling
they	will be feeling

Future II

I	will have	felt
you	will have	felt
he/she/it	will have	felt
we	will have	felt
you	will have	felt
they	will have	felt

Future II Continuous

I	will have been	feeling
you	will have been	feeling
he/she/it	will have been	feeling
we	will have been	feeling
you	will have been	feeling
they	will have been	feeling

IMPERATIVE
feel

GERUND
feeling

PAST PARTICIPLE
felt

CONDITIONAL

Conditional II

I	would	feel
you	would	feel
he/she/it	would	feel
we	would	feel
you	would	feel
they	would	feel

Conditional Past

I	would have	felt
you	would have	felt
he/she/it	would have	felt
we	would have	felt
you	would have	felt
they	would have	felt

IRREGULAR

FIND
achar

SIMPLE

Present Simple

I	find
you	find
he/she/it	finds
we	find
you	find
they	find

Past Simple

I	found
you	found
he/she/it	found
we	found
you	found
they	found

Present Perfect

I	have	found
you	have	found
he/she/it	has	found
we	have	found
you	have	found
they	have	found

Past Perfect

I	had	found
you	had	found
he/she/it	had	found
we	had	found
you	had	found
they	had	found

CONTINUOUS

Present Continuous

I	am	finding
you	are	finding
he/she/it	is	finding
we	are	finding
you	are	finding
they	are	finding

Past Continuous

I	was	finding
you	were	finding
he/she/it	was	finding
we	were	finding
you	were	finding
they	were	finding

Present Perfect Continuous

I	have been	finding
you	have been	finding
he/she/it	has been	finding
we	have been	finding
you	have been	finding
they	have been	finding

Past Perfect Continuous

I	had been	finding
you	had been	finding
he/she/it	had been	finding
we	had been	finding
you	had been	finding
they	had been	finding

FUTURE

Future I

I	will	find
you	will	find
he/she/it	will	find
we	will	find
you	will	find
they	will	find

Future I Continuous

I	will be finding
you	will be finding
he/she/it	will be finding
we	will be finding
you	will be finding
they	will be finding

Future II

I	will have	found
you	will have	found
he/she/it	will have	found
we	will have	found
you	will have	found
they	will have	found

Future II Continuous

I	will have been	finding
you	will have been	finding
he/she/it	will have been	finding
we	will have been	finding
you	will have been	finding
they	will have been	finding

IMPERATIVE
find

GERUND
finding

PAST PARTICIPLE
found

CONDITIONAL

Conditional II

I	would	find
you	would	find
he/she/it	would	find
we	would	find
you	would	find
they	would	find

Conditional Past

I	would have	found
you	would have	found
he/she/it	would have	found
we	would have	found
you	would have	found
they	would have	found

FLY

voar

-y → *-ie* antes de *-s* (ver p. 7)

SIMPLE

Present Simple

I	fly
you	fly
he/she/it	flies
we	fly
you	fly
they	fly

Past Simple

I	flew
you	flew
he/she/it	flew
we	flew
you	flew
they	flew

Present Perfect

I	have	flown
you	have	flown
he/she/it	has	flown
we	have	flown
you	have	flown
they	have	flown

Past Perfect

I	had	flown
you	had	flown
he/she/it	had	flown
we	had	flown
you	had	flown
they	had	flown

CONTINUOUS

Present Continuous

I	am	flying
you	are	flying
he/she/it	is	flying
we	are	flying
you	are	flying
they	are	flying

Past Continuous

I	was	flying
you	were	flying
he/she/it	was	flying
we	were	flying
you	were	flying
they	were	flying

Present Perfect Continuous

I	have been	flying
you	have been	flying
he/she/it	has been	flying
we	have been	flying
you	have been	flying
they	have been	flying

Past Perfect Continuous

I	had been	flying
you	had been	flying
he/she/it	had been	flying
we	had been	flying
you	had been	flying
they	had been	flying

FUTURE

Future I

I	will	fly
you	will	fly
he/she/it	will	fly
we	will	fly
you	will	fly
they	will	fly

Future I Continuous

I	will be flying
you	will be flying
he/she/it	will be flying
we	will be flying
you	will be flying
they	will be flying

Future II

I	will have	flown
you	will have	flown
he/she/it	will have	flown
we	will have	flown
you	will have	flown
they	will have	flown

Future II Continuous

I	will have been	flying
you	will have been	flying
he/she/it	will have been	flying
we	will have been	flying
you	will have been	flying
they	will have been	flying

IMPERATIVE

fly

GERUND

flying

PAST PARTICIPLE

flown

CONDITIONAL

Conditional II

I	would	fly
you	would	fly
he/she/it	would	fly
we	would	fly
you	would	fly
they	would	fly

Conditional Past

I	would have	flown
you	would have	flown
he/she/it	would have	flown
we	would have	flown
you	would have	flown
they	would have	flown

IRREGULAR

FORGET

esquecer

Duplicação de consoante (ver p. 7)

SIMPLE

Present Simple

I	forget
you	forget
he/she/it	forgets
we	forget
you	forget
they	forget

Past Simple

I	forgot
you	forgot
he/she/it	forgot
we	forgot
you	forgot
they	forgot

Present Perfect

I	have	forgotten
you	have	forgotten
he/she/it	has	forgotten
we	have	forgotten
you	have	forgotten
they	have	forgotten

Past Perfect

I	had	forgotten
you	had	forgotten
he/she/it	had	forgotten
we	had	forgotten
you	had	forgotten
they	had	forgotten

CONTINUOUS

Present Continuous

I	am	forgetting
you	are	forgetting
he/she/it	is	forgetting
we	are	forgetting
you	are	forgetting
they	are	forgetting

Past Continuous

I	was	forgetting
you	were	forgetting
he/she/it	was	forgetting
we	were	forgetting
you	were	forgetting
they	were	forgetting

Present Perfect Continuous

I	have been	forgetting
you	have been	forgetting
he/she/it	has been	forgetting
we	have been	forgetting
you	have been	forgetting
they	have been	forgetting

Past Perfect Continuous

I	had been	forgetting
you	had been	forgetting
he/she/it	had been	forgetting
we	had been	forgetting
you	had been	forgetting
they	had been	forgetting

FUTURE

Future I

I	will	forget
you	will	forget
he/she/it	will	forget
we	will	forget
you	will	forget
they	will	forget

Future I Continuous

I	will be forgetting
you	will be forgetting
he/she/it	will be forgetting
we	will be forgetting
you	will be forgetting
they	will be forgetting

Future II

I	will have forgotten
you	will have forgotten
he/she/it	will have forgotten
we	will have forgotten
you	will have forgotten
they	will have forgotten

Future II Continuous

I	will have been	forgetting
you	will have been	forgetting
he/she/it	will have been	forgetting
we	will have been	forgetting
you	will have been	forgetting
they	will have been	forgetting

IMPERATIVE

forget

GERUND

forgetting

PAST PARTICIPLE

forgotten

CONDITIONAL

Conditional II

I	would	forget
you	would	forget
he/she/it	would	forget
we	would	forget
you	would	forget
they	would	forget

Conditional Past

I	would have	forgotten
you	would have	forgotten
he/she/it	would have	forgotten
we	would have	forgotten
you	would have	forgotten
they	would have	forgotten

GET

obter, contrair (doença)

No IA o *Past Participle* é *gotten*.

SIMPLE

Present Simple

I	get
you	get
he/she/it	gets
we	get
you	get
they	get

Past Simple

I	got
you	got
he/she/it	got
we	got
you	got
they	got

Present Perfect

I	have	got
you	have	got
he/she/it	has	got
we	have	got
you	have	got
they	have	got

Past Perfect

I	had	got
you	had	got
he/she/it	had	got
we	had	got
you	had	got
they	had	got

CONTINUOUS

Present Continuous

I	am	getting
you	are	getting
he/she/it	is	getting
we	are	getting
you	are	getting
they	are	getting

Past Continuous

I	was	getting
you	were	getting
he/she/it	was	getting
we	were	getting
you	were	getting
they	were	getting

Present Perfect Continuous

I	have been	getting
you	have been	getting
he/she/it	has been	getting
we	have been	getting
you	have been	getting
they	have been	getting

Past Perfect Continuous

I	had been	getting
you	had been	getting
he/she/it	had been	getting
we	had been	getting
you	had been	getting
they	had been	getting

FUTURE

Future I

I	will	get
you	will	get
he/she/it	will	get
we	will	get
you	will	get
they	will	get

Future I Continuous

I	will be getting
you	will be getting
he/she/it	will be getting
we	will be getting
you	will be getting
they	will be getting

Future II

I	will have got
you	will have got
he/she/it	will have got
we	will have got
you	will have got
they	will have got

Future II Continuous

I	will have been getting
you	will have been getting
he/she/it	will have been getting
we	will have been getting
you	will have been getting
they	will have been getting

IMPERATIVE

get

GERUND

getting

PAST PARTICIPLE

got / gotten

CONDITIONAL

Conditional II

I	would	get
you	would	get
he/she/it	would	get
we	would	get
you	would	get
they	would	get

Conditional Past

I	would have	got
you	would have	got
he/she/it	would have	got
we	would have	got
you	would have	got
they	would have	got

IRREGULAR

GIVE
dar

+ *-ing* → ~~e~~ (ver p. 8)

SIMPLE

Present Simple

I	give
you	give
he/she/it	gives
we	give
you	give
they	give

Past Simple

I	**gave**
you	**gave**
he/she/it	**gave**
we	**gave**
you	**gave**
they	**gave**

Present Perfect

I	have	**given**
you	have	**given**
he/she/it	has	**given**
we	have	**given**
you	have	**given**
they	have	**given**

Past Perfect

I	had	**given**
you	had	**given**
he/she/it	had	**given**
we	had	**given**
you	had	**given**
they	had	**given**

CONTINUOUS

Present Continuous

I	am	giving
you	are	giving
he/she/it	is	giving
we	are	giving
you	are	giving
they	are	giving

Past Continuous

I	was	giving
you	were	giving
he/she/it	was	giving
we	were	giving
you	were	giving
they	were	giving

Present Perfect Continuous

I	have been	giving
you	have been	giving
he/she/it	has been	giving
we	have been	giving
you	have been	giving
they	have been	giving

Past Perfect Continuous

I	had been	giving
you	had been	giving
he/she/it	had been	giving
we	had been	giving
you	had been	giving
they	had been	giving

FUTURE

Future I

I	will	give
you	will	give
he/she/it	will	give
we	will	give
you	will	give
they	will	give

Future I Continuous

I	will be giving
you	will be giving
he/she/it	will be giving
we	will be giving
you	will be giving
they	will be giving

Future II

I	will have **given**
you	will have **given**
he/she/it	will have **given**
we	will have **given**
you	will have **given**
they	will have **given**

Future II Continuous

I	will have been	giving
you	will have been	giving
he/she/it	will have been	giving
we	will have been	giving
you	will have been	giving
they	will have been	giving

IMPERATIVE
give

GERUND
giving

PAST PARTICIPLE
given

CONDITIONAL

Conditional II

I	would	give
you	would	give
he/she/it	would	give
we	would	give
you	would	give
they	would	give

Conditional Past

I	would have	**given**
you	would have	**given**
he/she/it	would have	**given**
we	would have	**given**
you	would have	**given**
they	would have	**given**

GO
ir

+ -*es* na 3ª pessoa do singular do *Present Simple* (ver p. 7)

SIMPLE

Present Simple

I	go
you	go
he/she/it	goes
we	go
you	go
they	go

Past Simple

I	went
you	went
he/she/it	went
we	went
you	went
they	went

Present Perfect

I	have	gone
you	have	gone
he/she/it	has	gone
we	have	gone
you	have	gone
they	have	gone

Past Perfect

I	had	gone
you	had	gone
he/she/it	had	gone
we	had	gone
you	had	gone
they	had	gone

CONTINUOUS

Present Continuous

I	am	going
you	are	going
he/she/it	is	going
we	are	going
you	are	going
they	are	going

Past Continuous

I	was	going
you	were	going
he/she/it	was	going
we	were	going
you	were	going
they	were	going

Present Perfect Continuous

I	have been	going
you	have been	going
he/she/it	has been	going
we	have been	going
you	have been	going
they	have been	going

Past Perfect Continuous

I	had been	going
you	had been	going
he/she/it	had been	going
we	had been	going
you	had been	going
they	had been	going

FUTURE

Future I

I	will	go
you	will	go
he/she/it	will	go
we	will	go
you	will	go
they	will	go

Future I Continuous

I	will be going
you	will be going
he/she/it	will be going
we	will be going
you	will be going
they	will be going

Future II

I	will have	gone
you	will have	gone
he/she/it	will have	gone
we	will have	gone
you	will have	gone
they	will have	gone

Future II Continuous

I	will have been	going
you	will have been	going
he/she/it	will have been	going
we	will have been	going
you	will have been	going
they	will have been	going

IMPERATIVE
go

GERUND
going

PAST PARTICIPLE
gone

CONDITIONAL

Conditional II

I	would	go
you	would	go
he/she/it	would	go
we	would	go
you	would	go
they	would	go

Conditional Past

I	would have	gone
you	would have	gone
he/she/it	would have	gone
we	would have	gone
you	would have	gone
they	would have	gone

IRREGULAR
TAMBÉM VERBO AUXILIAR

HAVE
ter

+ *-ing* → ~~e~~ (ver p. 8)

SIMPLE

Present Simple

I	have
you	have
he/she/it	has
we	have
you	have
they	have

Past Simple

I	had
you	had
he/she/it	had
we	had
you	had
they	had

Present Perfect

I	have	had
you	have	had
he/she/it	has	had
we	have	had
you	have	had
they	have	had

Past Perfect

I	had	had
you	had	had
he/she/it	had	had
we	had	had
you	had	had
they	had	had

CONTINUOUS

Present Continuous

I	am	having
you	are	having
he/she/it	is	having
we	are	having
you	are	having
they	are	having

Past Continuous

I	was	having
you	were	having
he/she/it	was	having
we	were	having
you	were	having
they	were	having

Present Perfect Continuous

I	have been	having
you	have been	having
he/she/it	has been	having
we	have been	having
you	have been	having
they	have been	having

Past Perfect Continuous

I	had been	having
you	had been	having
he/she/it	had been	having
we	had been	having
you	had been	having
they	had been	having

FUTURE

Future I

I	will	have
you	will	have
he/she/it	will	have
we	will	have
you	will	have
they	will	have

Future I Continuous

I	will be having
you	will be having
he/she/it	will be having
we	will be having
you	will be having
they	will be having

Future II

I	will have	had
you	will have	had
he/she/it	will have	had
we	will have	had
you	will have	had
they	will have	had

Future II Continuous

I	will have been	having
you	will have been	having
he/she/it	will have been	having
we	will have been	having
you	will have been	having
they	will have been	having

IMPERATIVE
have

GERUND
having

PAST PARTICIPLE
had

CONDITIONAL

Conditional II

I	would	have
you	would	have
he/she/it	would	have
we	would	have
you	would	have
they	would	have

Conditional Past

I	would have	had
you	would have	had
he/she/it	would have	had
we	would have	had
you	would have	had
they	would have	had

HEAR
ouvir

SIMPLE

Present Simple

I	hear
you	hear
he/she/it	hears
we	hear
you	hear
they	hear

Past Simple

I	heard
you	heard
he/she/it	heard
we	heard
you	heard
they	heard

Present Perfect

I	have	heard
you	have	heard
he/she/it	has	heard
we	have	heard
you	have	heard
they	have	heard

Past Perfect

I	had	heard
you	had	heard
he/she/it	had	heard
we	had	heard
you	had	heard
they	had	heard

CONTINUOUS

Present Continuous

I	am	hearing
you	are	hearing
he/she/it	is	hearing
we	are	hearing
you	are	hearing
they	are	hearing

Past Continuous

I	was	hearing
you	were	hearing
he/she/it	was	hearing
we	were	hearing
you	were	hearing
they	were	hearing

Present Perfect Continuous

I	have been	hearing
you	have been	hearing
he/she/it	has been	hearing
we	have been	hearing
you	have been	hearing
they	have been	hearing

Past Perfect Continuous

I	had been	hearing
you	had been	hearing
he/she/it	had been	hearing
we	had been	hearing
you	had been	hearing
they	had been	hearing

FUTURE

Future I

I	will	hear
you	will	hear
he/she/it	will	hear
we	will	hear
you	will	hear
they	will	hear

Future I Continuous

I	will be hearing
you	will be hearing
he/she/it	will be hearing
we	will be hearing
you	will be hearing
they	will be hearing

Future II

I	will have	heard
you	will have	heard
he/she/it	will have	heard
we	will have	heard
you	will have	heard
they	will have	heard

Future II Continuous

I	will have been	hearing
you	will have been	hearing
he/she/it	will have been	hearing
we	will have been	hearing
you	will have been	hearing
they	will have been	hearing

IMPERATIVE
hear

GERUND
hearing

PAST PARTICIPLE
heard

CONDITIONAL

Conditional II

I	would	hear
you	would	hear
he/she/it	would	hear
we	would	hear
you	would	hear
they	would	hear

Conditional Past

I	would have	heard
you	would have	heard
he/she/it	would have	heard
we	would have	heard
you	would have	heard
they	would have	heard

HELP
ajudar

SIMPLE

Present Simple

I	help
you	help
he/she/it	helps
we	help
you	help
they	help

Past Simple

I	helped
you	helped
he/she/it	helped
we	helped
you	helped
they	helped

Present Perfect

I	have	helped
you	have	helped
he/she/it	has	helped
we	have	helped
you	have	helped
they	have	helped

Past Perfect

I	had	helped
you	had	helped
he/she/it	had	helped
we	had	helped
you	had	helped
they	had	helped

CONTINUOUS

Present Continuous

I	am	helping
you	are	helping
he/she/it	is	helping
we	are	helping
you	are	helping
they	are	helping

Past Continuous

I	was	helping
you	were	helping
he/she/it	was	helping
we	were	helping
you	were	helping
they	were	helping

Present Perfect Continuous

I	have been	helping
you	have been	helping
he/she/it	has been	helping
we	have been	helping
you	have been	helping
they	have been	helping

Past Perfect Continuous

I	had been	helping
you	had been	helping
he/she/it	had been	helping
we	had been	helping
you	had been	helping
they	had been	helping

FUTURE

Future I

I	will	help
you	will	help
he/she/it	will	help
we	will	help
you	will	help
they	will	help

Future I Continuous

I	will be helping
you	will be helping
he/she/it	will be helping
we	will be helping
you	will be helping
they	will be helping

Future II

I	will have	helped
you	will have	helped
he/she/it	will have	helped
we	will have	helped
you	will have	helped
they	will have	helped

Future II Continuous

I	will have been	helping
you	will have been	helping
he/she/it	will have been	helping
we	will have been	helping
you	will have been	helping
they	will have been	helping

IMPERATIVE
help

GERUND
helping

PAST PARTICIPLE
helped

CONDITIONAL

Conditional II

I	would	help
you	would	help
he/she/it	would	help
we	would	help
you	would	help
they	would	help

Conditional Past

I	would have	helped
you	would have	helped
he/she/it	would have	helped
we	would have	helped
you	would have	helped
they	would have	helped

HIT
bater

Duplicação de consoante (ver p. 7)

SIMPLE

Present Simple

I	hit
you	hit
he/she/it	hits
we	hit
you	hit
they	hit

Past Simple

I	hit
you	hit
he/she/it	hit
we	hit
you	hit
they	hit

Present Perfect

I	have	hit
you	have	hit
he/she/it	has	hit
we	have	hit
you	have	hit
they	have	hit

Past Perfect

I	had	hit
you	had	hit
he/she/it	had	hit
we	had	hit
you	had	hit
they	had	hit

CONTINUOUS

Present Continuous

I	am	hitting
you	are	hitting
he/she/it	is	hitting
we	are	hitting
you	are	hitting
they	are	hitting

Past Continuous

I	was	hitting
you	were	hitting
he/she/it	was	hitting
we	were	hitting
you	were	hitting
they	were	hitting

Present Perfect Continuous

I	have been	hitting
you	have been	hitting
he/she/it	has been	hitting
we	have been	hitting
you	have been	hitting
they	have been	hitting

Past Perfect Continuous

I	had been	hitting
you	had been	hitting
he/she/it	had been	hitting
we	had been	hitting
you	had been	hitting
they	had been	hitting

FUTURE

Future I

I	will	hit
you	will	hit
he/she/it	will	hit
we	will	hit
you	will	hit
they	will	hit

Future I Continuous

I	will be hitting
you	will be hitting
he/she/it	will be hitting
we	will be hitting
you	will be hitting
they	will be hitting

Future II

I	will have	hit
you	will have	hit
he/she/it	will have	hit
we	will have	hit
you	will have	hit
they	will have	hit

Future II Continuous

I	will have been	hitting
you	will have been	hitting
he/she/it	will have been	hitting
we	will have been	hitting
you	will have been	hitting
they	will have been	hitting

IMPERATIVE
hit

GERUND
hitting

PAST PARTICIPLE
hit

CONDITIONAL

Conditional II

I	would	hit
you	would	hit
he/she/it	would	hit
we	would	hit
you	would	hit
they	would	hit

Conditional Past

I	would have	hit
you	would have	hit
he/she/it	would have	hit
we	would have	hit
you	would have	hit
they	would have	hit

HURT
machucar

SIMPLE

Present Simple

I	hurt
you	hurt
he/she/it	hurts
we	hurt
you	hurt
they	hurt

Past Simple

I	hurt
you	hurt
he/she/it	hurt
we	hurt
you	hurt
they	hurt

Present Perfect

I	have	hurt
you	have	hurt
he/she/it	has	hurt
we	have	hurt
you	have	hurt
they	have	hurt

Past Perfect

I	had	hurt
you	had	hurt
he/she/it	had	hurt
we	had	hurt
you	had	hurt
they	had	hurt

CONTINUOUS

Present Continuous

I	am	hurting
you	are	hurting
he/she/it	is	hurting
we	are	hurting
you	are	hurting
they	are	hurting

Past Continuous

I	was	hurting
you	were	hurting
he/she/it	was	hurting
we	were	hurting
you	were	hurting
they	were	hurting

Present Perfect Continuous

I	have been	hurting
you	have been	hurting
he/she/it	has been	hurting
we	have been	hurting
you	have been	hurting
they	have been	hurting

Past Perfect Continuous

I	had	been	hurting
you	had	been	hurting
he/she/it	had	been	hurting
we	had	been	hurting
you	had	been	hurting
they	had	been	hurting

FUTURE

Future I

I	will	hurt
you	will	hurt
he/she/it	will	hurt
we	will	hurt
you	will	hurt
they	will	hurt

Future I Continuous

I	will be hurting
you	will be hurting
he/she/it	will be hurting
we	will be hurting
you	will be hurting
they	will be hurting

Future II

I	will have	hurt
you	will have	hurt
he/she/it	will have	hurt
we	will have	hurt
you	will have	hurt
they	will have	hurt

Future II Continuous

I	will have been	hurting
you	will have been	hurting
he/she/it	will have been	hurting
we	will have been	hurting
you	will have been	hurting
they	will have been	hurting

IMPERATIVE
hurt

GERUND
hurting

PAST PARTICIPLE
hurt

CONDITIONAL

Conditional II

I	would	hurt
you	would	hurt
he/she/it	would	hurt
we	would	hurt
you	would	hurt
they	would	hurt

Conditional Past

I	would have	hurt
you	would have	hurt
he/she/it	would have	hurt
we	would have	hurt
you	would have	hurt
they	would have	hurt

INVITE
convidar

+ *-ing* → ~~e~~ (ver p. 8) / + *-d* não *-ed* (ver p. 7)

SIMPLE

Present Simple

I	invite
you	invite
he/she/it	invites
we	invite
you	invite
they	invite

Past Simple

I	invited
you	invited
he/she/it	invited
we	invited
you	invited
they	invited

Present Perfect

I	have	invited
you	have	invited
he/she/it	has	invited
we	have	invited
you	have	invited
they	have	invited

Past Perfect

I	had	invited
you	had	invited
he/she/it	had	invited
we	had	invited
you	had	invited
they	had	invited

CONTINUOUS

Present Continuous

I	am	inviting
you	are	inviting
he/she/it	is	inviting
we	are	inviting
you	are	inviting
they	are	inviting

Past Continuous

I	was	inviting
you	were	inviting
he/she/it	was	inviting
we	were	inviting
you	were	inviting
they	were	inviting

Present Perfect Continuous

I	have	been	inviting
you	have	been	inviting
he/she/it	has	been	inviting
we	have	been	inviting
you	have	been	inviting
they	have	been	inviting

Past Perfect Continuous

I	had	been	inviting
you	had	been	inviting
he/she/it	had	been	inviting
we	had	been	inviting
you	had	been	inviting
they	had	been	inviting

FUTURE

Future I

I	will	invite
you	will	invite
he/she/it	will	invite
we	will	invite
you	will	invite
they	will	invite

Future I Continuous

I	will be inviting
you	will be inviting
he/she/it	will be inviting
we	will be inviting
you	will be inviting
they	will be inviting

Future II

I	will have	invited
you	will have	invited
he/she/it	will have	invited
we	will have	invited
you	will have	invited
they	will have	invited

Future II Continuous

I	will have been	inviting
you	will have been	inviting
he/she/it	will have been	inviting
we	will have been	inviting
you	will have been	inviting
they	will have been	inviting

IMPERATIVE
invite

GERUND
inviting

PAST PARTICIPLE
invited

CONDITIONAL

Conditional II

I	would	invite
you	would	invite
he/she/it	would	invite
we	would	invite
you	would	invite
they	would	invite

Conditional Past

I	would have	invited
you	would have	invited
he/she/it	would have	invited
we	would have	invited
you	would have	invited
they	would have	invited

IRREGULAR

KNOW

saber, conhecer

Know não tem forma contínua.

SIMPLE

Present Simple

I	know
you	know
he/she/it	knows
we	know
you	know
they	know

Past Simple

I	knew
you	knew
he/she/it	knew
we	knew
you	knew
they	knew

Present Perfect

I	have	known
you	have	known
he/she/it	has	known
we	have	known
you	have	known
they	have	known

Past Perfect

I	had	known
you	had	known
he/she/it	had	known
we	had	known
you	had	known
they	had	known

CONTINUOUS

Present Continuous

—

Past Continuous

—

Present Perfect Continuous

—

Past Perfect Continuous

—

FUTURE

Future I

I	will	know
you	will	know
he/she/it	will	know
we	will	know
you	will	know
they	will	know

Future I Continuous

—

Future II

I	will have	known
you	will have	known
he/she/it	will have	known
we	will have	known
you	will have	known
they	will have	known

Future II Continuous

—

IMPERATIVE

know

GERUND

knowing

PAST PARTICIPLE

known

CONDITIONAL

Conditional II

I	would	know
you	would	know
he/she/it	would	know
we	would	know
you	would	know
they	would	know

Conditional Past

I	would have	known
you	would have	known
he/she/it	would have	known
we	would have	known
you	would have	known
they	would have	known

LEARN

aprender

No IA o *Past Participle* é *learned*.

SIMPLE

Present Simple

I	learn
you	learn
he/she/it	learns
we	learn
you	learn
they	learn

Past Simple

I	learnt
you	learnt
he/she/it	learnt
we	learnt
you	learnt
they	learnt

Present Perfect

I	have	learnt
you	have	learnt
he/she/it	has	learnt
we	have	learnt
you	have	learnt
they	have	learnt

Past Perfect

I	had	learnt
you	had	learnt
he/she/it	had	learnt
we	had	learnt
you	had	learnt
they	had	learnt

CONTINUOUS

Present Continuous

I	am	learning
you	are	learning
he/she/it	is	learning
we	are	learning
you	are	learning
they	are	learning

Past Continuous

I	was	learning
you	were	learning
he/she/it	was	learning
we	were	learning
you	were	learning
they	were	learning

Present Perfect Continuous

I	have	been	learning
you	have	been	learning
he/she/it	has	been	learning
we	have	been	learning
you	have	been	learning
they	have	been	learning

Past Perfect Continuous

I	had	been	learning
you	had	been	learning
he/she/it	had	been	learning
we	had	been	learning
you	had	been	learning
they	had	been	learning

FUTURE

Future I

I	will	learn
you	will	learn
he/she/it	will	learn
we	will	learn
you	will	learn
they	will	learn

Future I Continuous

I	will be learning
you	will be learning
he/she/it	will be learning
we	will be learning
you	will be learning
they	will be learning

Future II

I	will have	learnt
you	will have	learnt
he/she/it	will have	learnt
we	will have	learnt
you	will have	learnt
they	will have	learnt

Future II Continuous

I	will have been	learning
you	will have been	learning
he/she/it	will have been	learning
we	will have been	learning
you	will have been	learning
they	will have been	learning

IMPERATIVE

learn

GERUND

learning

PAST PARTICIPLE

learnt / learned

CONDITIONAL

Conditional II

I	would	learn
you	would	learn
he/she/it	would	learn
we	would	learn
you	would	learn
they	would	learn

Conditional Past

I	would have	learnt
you	would have	learnt
he/she/it	would have	learnt
we	would have	learnt
you	would have	learnt
they	would have	learnt

IRREGULAR

LEAVE

deixar, abandonar

+ *-ing* → ~~e~~ (ver p. 8)

SIMPLE

Present Simple

I	leave
you	leave
he/she/it	leaves
we	leave
you	leave
they	leave

Past Simple

I	left
you	left
he/she/it	left
we	left
you	left
they	left

Present Perfect

I	have	left
you	have	left
he/she/it	has	left
we	have	left
you	have	left
they	have	left

Past Perfect

I	had	left
you	had	left
he/she/it	had	left
we	had	left
you	had	left
they	had	left

CONTINUOUS

Present Continuous

I	am	leaving
you	are	leaving
he/she/it	is	leaving
we	are	leaving
you	are	leaving
they	are	leaving

Past Continuous

I	was	leaving
you	were	leaving
he/she/it	was	leaving
we	were	leaving
you	were	leaving
they	were	leaving

Present Perfect Continuous

I	have been	leaving
you	have been	leaving
he/she/it	has been	leaving
we	have been	leaving
you	have been	leaving
they	have been	leaving

Past Perfect Continuous

I	had been	leaving
you	had been	leaving
he/she/it	had been	leaving
we	had been	leaving
you	had been	leaving
they	had been	leaving

FUTURE

Future I

I	will	leave
you	will	leave
he/she/it	will	leave
we	will	leave
you	will	leave
they	will	leave

Future I Continuous

I	will be leaving
you	will be leaving
he/she/it	will be leaving
we	will be leaving
you	will be leaving
they	will be leaving

Future II

I	will have left
you	will have left
he/she/it	will have left
we	will have left
you	will have left
they	will have left

Future II Continuous

I	will have been	leaving
you	will have been	leaving
he/she/it	will have been	leaving
we	will have been	leaving
you	will have been	leaving
they	will have been	leaving

IMPERATIVE
leave

GERUND
leaving

PAST PARTICIPLE
left

CONDITIONAL

Conditional II

I	would	leave
you	would	leave
he/she/it	would	leave
we	would	leave
you	would	leave
they	would	leave

Conditional Past

I	would have	left
you	would have	left
he/she/it	would have	left
we	would have	left
you	would have	left
they	would have	left

LEND
empréstar

SIMPLE

Present Simple

I	lend
you	lend
he/she/it	lends
we	lend
you	lend
they	lend

Past Simple

I	lent
you	lent
he/she/it	lent
we	lent
you	lent
they	lent

Present Perfect

I	have	lent
you	have	lent
he/she/it	has	lent
we	have	lent
you	have	lent
they	have	lent

Past Perfect

I	had	lent
you	had	lent
he/she/it	had	lent
we	had	lent
you	had	lent
they	had	lent

CONTINUOUS

Present Continuous

I	am	lending
you	are	lending
he/she/it	is	lending
we	are	lending
you	are	lending
they	are	lending

Past Continuous

I	was	lending
you	were	lending
he/she/it	was	lending
we	were	lending
you	were	lending
they	were	lending

Present Perfect Continuous

I	have been	lending
you	have been	lending
he/she/it	has been	lending
we	have been	lending
you	have been	lending
they	have been	lending

Past Perfect Continuous

I	had been	lending
you	had been	lending
he/she/it	had been	lending
we	had been	lending
you	had been	lending
they	had been	lending

FUTURE

Future I

I	will	lend
you	will	lend
he/she/it	will	lend
we	will	lend
you	will	lend
they	will	lend

Future I Continuous

I	will be lending
you	will be lending
he/she/it	will be lending
we	will be lending
you	will be lending
they	will be lending

Future II

I	will have lent
you	will have lent
he/she/it	will have lent
we	will have lent
you	will have lent
they	will have lent

Future II Continuous

I	will have been	lending
you	will have been	lending
he/she/it	will have been	lending
we	will have been	lending
you	will have been	lending
they	will have been	lending

IMPERATIVE
lend

GERUND
lending

PAST PARTICIPLE
lent

CONDITIONAL

Conditional II

I	would	lend
you	would	lend
he/she/it	would	lend
we	would	lend
you	would	lend
they	would	lend

Conditional Past

I	would have lent
you	would have lent
he/she/it	would have lent
we	would have lent
you	would have lent
they	would have lent

REGULAR

LIKE

gostar

Like não tem forma contínua.

SIMPLE

Present Simple

I	like
you	like
he/she/it	likes
we	like
you	like
they	like

Past Simple

I	liked
you	liked
he/she/it	liked
we	liked
you	liked
they	liked

Present Perfect

I	have	liked
you	have	liked
he/she/it	has	liked
we	have	liked
you	have	liked
they	have	liked

Past Perfect

I	had	liked
you	had	liked
he/she/it	had	liked
we	had	liked
you	had	liked
they	had	liked

CONTINUOUS

Present Continuous

—

Past Continuous

—

Present Perfect Continuous

—

Past Perfect Continuous

—

FUTURE

Future I

I	will	like
you	will	like
he/she/it	will	like
we	will	like
you	will	like
they	will	like

Future I Continuous

—

Future II

I	will have	liked
you	will have	liked
he/she/it	will have	liked
we	will have	liked
you	will have	liked
they	will have	liked

Future II Continuous

—

IMPERATIVE

like

GERUND

liking

PAST PARTICIPLE

liked

CONDITIONAL

Conditional II

I	would	like
you	would	like
he/she/it	would	like
we	would	like
you	would	like
they	would	like

Conditional Past

I	would have	liked
you	would have	liked
he/she/it	would have	liked
we	would have	liked
you	would have	liked
they	would have	liked

LISTEN
escutar

SIMPLE

Present Simple

I	listen
you	listen
he/she/it	listens
we	listen
you	listen
they	listen

Past Simple

I	listened
you	listened
he/she/it	listened
we	listened
you	listened
they	listened

Present Perfect

I	have	listened
you	have	listened
he/she/it	has	listened
we	have	listened
you	have	listened
they	have	listened

Past Perfect

I	had	listened
you	had	listened
he/she/it	had	listened
we	had	listened
you	had	listened
they	had	listened

CONTINUOUS

Present Continuous

I	am	listening
you	are	listening
he/she/it	is	listening
we	are	listening
you	are	listening
they	are	listening

Past Continuous

I	was	listening
you	were	listening
he/she/it	was	listening
we	were	listening
you	were	listening
they	were	listening

Present Perfect Continuous

I	have	been	listening
you	have	been	listening
he/she/it	has	been	listening
we	have	been	listening
you	have	been	listening
they	have	been	listening

Past Perfect Continuous

I	had	been	listening
you	had	been	listening
he/she/it	had	been	listening
we	had	been	listening
you	had	been	listening
they	had	been	listening

FUTURE

Future I

II	will	listen
you	will	listen
he/she/it	will	listen
we	will	listen
you	will	listen
they	will	listen

Future I Continuous

I	will be listening
you	will be listening
he/she/it	will be listening
we	will be listening
you	will be listening
they	will be listening

Future II

I	will have	listened
you	will have	listened
he/she/it	will have	listened
we	will have	listened
you	will have	listened
they	will have	listened

Future II Continuous

I	will have been	listening
you	will have been	listening
he/she/it	will have been	listening
we	will have been	listening
you	will have been	listening
they	will have been	listening

IMPERATIVE
listen

GERUND
listening

PAST PARTICIPLE
listened

CONDITIONAL

Conditional II

I	would	listen
you	would	listen
he/she/it	would	listen
we	would	listen
you	would	listen
they	would	listen

Conditional Past

I	would have	listened
you	would have	listened
he/she/it	would have	listened
we	would have	listened
you	would have	listened
they	would have	listened

REGULAR

LIVE

viver, morar

+ ***-ing*** → ~~e~~ (ver p. 8) / + ***-d*** não ***-ed*** (ver p. 7)

SIMPLE

Present Simple

I	live
you	live
he/she/it	lives
we	live
you	live
they	live

Past Simple

I	lived
you	lived
he/she/it	lived
we	lived
you	lived
they	lived

Present Perfect

I	have	lived
you	have	lived
he/she/it	has	lived
we	have	lived
you	have	lived
they	have	lived

Past Perfect

I	had	lived
you	had	lived
he/she/it	had	lived
we	had	lived
you	had	lived
they	had	lived

CONTINUOUS

Present Continuous

I	am	living
you	are	living
he/she/it	is	living
we	are	living
you	are	living
they	are	living

Past Continuous

I	was	living
you	were	living
he/she/it	was	living
we	were	living
you	were	living
they	were	living

Present Perfect Continuous

I	have been	living
you	have been	living
he/she/it	has been	living
we	have been	living
you	have been	living
they	have been	living

Past Perfect Continuous

I	had	been	living
you	had	been	living
he/she/it	had	been	living
we	had	been	living
you	had	been	living
they	had	been	living

FUTURE

Future I

I	will	live
you	will	live
he/she/it	will	live
we	will	live
you	will	live
they	will	live

Future I Continuous

I	will be living
you	will be living
he/she/it	will be living
we	will be living
you	will be living
they	will be living

Future II

I	will have	lived
you	will have	lived
he/she/it	will have	lived
we	will have	lived
you	will have	lived
they	will have	lived

Future II Continuous

I	will have been	living
you	will have been	living
he/she/it	will have been	living
we	will have been	living
you	will have been	living
they	will have been	living

IMPERATIVE

live

GERUND

living

PAST PARTICIPLE

lived

CONDITIONAL

Conditional II

I	would	live
you	would	live
he/she/it	would	live
we	would	live
you	would	live
they	would	live

Conditional Past

I	would have	lived
you	would have	lived
he/she/it	would have	lived
we	would have	lived
you	would have	lived
they	would have	lived

LOOK
olhar

SIMPLE

Present Simple

I	look
you	look
he/she/it	looks
we	look
you	look
they	look

Past Simple

I	looked
you	looked
he/she/it	looked
we	looked
you	looked
they	looked

Present Perfect

I	have	looked
you	have	looked
he/she/it	has	looked
we	have	looked
you	have	looked
they	have	looked

Past Perfect

I	had	looked
you	had	looked
he/she/it	had	looked
we	had	looked
you	had	looked
they	had	looked

CONTINUOUS

Present Continuous

I	am	looking
you	are	looking
he/she/it	is	looking
we	are	looking
you	are	looking
they	are	looking

Past Continuous

I	was	looking
you	were	looking
he/she/it	was	looking
we	were	looking
you	were	looking
they	were	looking

Present Perfect Continuous

I	have been	looking
you	have been	looking
he/she/it	has been	looking
we	have been	looking
you	have been	looking
they	have been	looking

Past Perfect Continuous

I	had been	looking
you	had been	looking
he/she/it	had been	looking
we	had been	looking
you	had been	looking
they	had been	looking

FUTURE

Future I

I	will	look
you	will	look
he/she/it	will	look
we	will	look
you	will	look
they	will	look

Future I Continuous

I	will be looking
you	will be looking
he/she/it	will be looking
we	will be looking
you	will be looking
they	will be looking

Future II

I	will have	looked
you	will have	looked
he/she/it	will have	looked
we	will have	looked
you	will have	looked
they	will have	looked

Future II Continuous

I	will have been	looking
you	will have been	looking
he/she/it	will have been	looking
we	will have been	looking
you	will have been	looking
they	will have been	looking

IMPERATIVE
look

GERUND
looking

PAST PARTICIPLE
looked

CONDITIONAL

Conditional II

I	would	look
you	would	look
he/she/it	would	look
we	would	look
you	would	look
they	would	look

Conditional Past

I	would have	looked
you	would have	looked
he/she/it	would have	looked
we	would have	looked
you	would have	looked
they	would have	looked

LOSE

perder

+ ***-ing*** → ~~e~~ (ver p. 8)

SIMPLE

Present Simple

I	lose
you	lose
he/she/it	lose**s**
we	lose
you	lose
they	lose

Past Simple

I	**lost**
you	**lost**
he/she/it	**lost**
we	**lost**
you	**lost**
they	**lost**

Present Perfect

I	have	**lost**
you	have	**lost**
he/she/it	has	**lost**
we	have	**lost**
you	have	**lost**
they	have	**lost**

Past Perfect

I	had	**lost**
you	had	**lost**
he/she/it	had	**lost**
we	had	**lost**
you	had	**lost**
they	had	**lost**

CONTINUOUS

Present Continuous

I	am	losing
you	are	losing
he/she/it	is	losing
we	are	losing
you	are	losing
they	are	losing

Past Continuous

I	was	losing
you	were	losing
he/she/it	was	losing
we	were	losing
you	were	losing
they	were	losing

Present Perfect Continuous

I	have been	losing
you	have been	losing
he/she/it	has been	losing
we	have been	losing
you	have been	losing
they	have been	losing

Past Perfect Continuous

I	had been	losing
you	had been	losing
he/she/it	had been	losing
we	had been	losing
you	had been	losing
they	had been	losing

FUTURE

Future I

I	will	lose
you	will	lose
he/she/it	will	lose
we	will	lose
you	will	lose
they	will	lose

Future I Continuous

I	will be losing
you	will be losing
he/she/it	will be losing
we	will be losing
you	will be losing
they	will be losing

Future II

I	will have **lost**
you	will have **lost**
he/she/it	will have **lost**
we	will have **lost**
you	will have **lost**
they	will have **lost**

Future II Continuous

I	will have been	losing
you	will have been	losing
he/she/it	will have been	losing
we	will have been	losing
you	will have been	losing
they	will have been	losing

IMPERATIVE

lose

GERUND

losing

PAST PARTICIPLE

lost

CONDITIONAL

Conditional II

I	would	lose
you	would	lose
he/she/it	would	lose
we	would	lose
you	would	lose
they	would	lose

Conditional Past

I	would have	**lost**
you	would have	**lost**
he/she/it	would have	**lost**
we	would have	**lost**
you	would have	**lost**
they	would have	**lost**

MAKE
fazer

+ *-ing* → ~~e~~ (ver p. 8)

SIMPLE

Present Simple

I	make
you	make
he/she/it	makes
we	make
you	make
they	make

Past Simple

I	**made**
you	**made**
he/she/it	**made**
we	**made**
you	**made**
they	**made**

Present Perfect

I	have	**made**
you	have	**made**
he/she/it	has	**made**
we	have	**made**
you	have	**made**
they	have	**made**

Past Perfect

I	had	**made**
you	had	**made**
he/she/it	had	**made**
we	had	**made**
you	had	**made**
they	had	**made**

CONTINUOUS

Present Continuous

I	am	making
you	are	making
he/she/it	is	making
we	are	making
you	are	making
they	are	making

Past Continuous

I	was	making
you	were	making
he/she/it	was	making
we	were	making
you	were	making
they	were	making

Present Perfect Continuous

I	have been	making
you	have been	making
he/she/it	has been	making
we	have been	making
you	have been	making
they	have been	making

Past Perfect Continuous

I	had been	making
you	had been	making
he/she/it	had been	making
we	had been	making
you	had been	making
they	had been	making

FUTURE

Future I

I	will	make
you	will	make
he/she/it	will	make
we	will	make
you	will	make
they	will	make

Future I Continuous

I	will be making
you	will be making
he/she/it	will be making
we	will be making
you	will be making
they	will be making

Future II

I	will have **made**
you	will have **made**
he/she/it	will have **made**
we	will have **made**
you	will have **made**
they	will have **made**

Future II Continuous

I	will have been	making
you	will have been	making
he/she/it	will have been	making
we	will have been	making
you	will have been	making
they	will have been	making

IMPERATIVE
make

GERUND
making

PAST PARTICIPLE
made

CONDITIONAL

Conditional II

I	would	make
you	would	make
he/she/it	would	make
we	would	make
you	would	make
they	would	make

Conditional Past

I	would have	**made**
you	would have	**made**
he/she/it	would have	**made**
we	would have	**made**
you	would have	**made**
they	would have	**made**

IRREGULAR

MEET
encontrar

SIMPLE

Present Simple

I	meet
you	meet
he/she/it	meets
we	meet
you	meet
they	meet

Past Simple

I	met
you	met
he/she/it	met
we	met
you	met
they	met

Present Perfect

I	have	met
you	have	met
he/she/it	has	met
we	have	met
you	have	met
they	have	met

Past Perfect

I	had	met
you	had	met
he/she/it	had	met
we	had	met
you	had	met
they	had	met

CONTINUOUS

Present Continuous

I	am	meeting
you	are	meeting
he/she/it	is	meeting
we	are	meeting
you	are	meeting
they	are	meeting

Past Continuous

I	was	meeting
you	were	meeting
he/she/it	was	meeting
we	were	meeting
you	were	meeting
they	were	meeting

Present Perfect Continuous

I	have been	meeting
you	have been	meeting
he/she/it	has been	meeting
we	have been	meeting
you	have been	meeting
they	have been	meeting

Past Perfect Continuous

I	had	been	meeting
you	had	been	meeting
he/she/it	had	been	meeting
we	had	been	meeting
you	had	been	meeting
they	had	been	meeting

FUTURE

Future I

I	will	meet
you	will	meet
he/she/it	will	meet
we	will	meet
you	will	meet
they	will	meet

Future I Continuous

I	will be meeting
you	will be meeting
he/she/it	will be meeting
we	will be meeting
you	will be meeting
they	will be meeting

Future II

I	will have	met
you	will have	met
he/she/it	will have	met
we	will have	met
you	will have	met
they	will have	met

Future II Continuous

I	will have been	meeting
you	will have been	meeting
he/she/it	will have been	meeting
we	will have been	meeting
you	will have been	meeting
they	will have been	meeting

IMPERATIVE
meet

GERUND
meeting

PAST PARTICIPLE
met

CONDITIONAL

Conditional II

I	would	meet
you	would	meet
he/she/it	would	meet
we	would	meet
you	would	meet
they	would	meet

Conditional Past

I	would have	met
you	would have	met
he/she/it	would have	met
we	would have	met
you	would have	met
they	would have	met

MUST / HAVE TO

precisar / ter de

Must só pode ser empregado no *Infinitive*. Nos demais tempos emprega-se *have to*. / *Have to* no *Present Continuous* e no *Past Continuous* emprega-se freqüentemente com *always* e tem uma conotação negativa.

SIMPLE

Present Simple

I	must / have to
you	must / have to
he/she/it	must / has to
we	must / have to
you	must / have to
they	must / have to

Past Simple

I	had to
you	had to
he/she/it	had to
we	had to
you	had to
they	had to

Present Perfect

I	have	had to
you	have	had to
he/she/it	has	had to
we	have	had to
you	have	had to
they	have	had to

Past Perfect

I	had	had to
you	had	had to
he/she/it	had	had to
we	had	had to
you	had	had to
they	had	had to

CONTINUOUS

Present Continuous

I	am	having to
you	are	having to
he/she/it	is	having to
we	are	having to
you	are	having to
they	are	having to

Past Continuous

I	was	having to
you	were	having to
he/she/it	was	having to
we	were	having to
you	were	having to
they	were	having to

Present Perfect Continuous

I	have been	having to
you	have been	having to
he/she/it	has been	having to
we	have been	having to
you	have been	having to
they	have been	having to

Past Perfect Continuous

I	had been	having to
you	had been	having to
he/she/it	had been	having to
we	had been	having to
you	had been	having to
they	had been	having to

FUTURE

Future I

I	will	have to
you	will	have to
he/she/it	will	have to
we	will	have to
you	will	have to
they	will	have to

Future I Continuous

I	will be having to
you	will be having to
he/she/it	will be having to
we	will be having to
you	will be having to
they	will be having to

Future II

I	will have	had to
you	will have	had to
he/she/it	will have	had to
we	will have	had to
you	will have	had to
they	will have	had to

Future II Continuous

I	will have been	having to
you	will have been	having to
he/she/it	will have been	having to
we	will have been	having to
you	will have been	having to
they	will have been	having to

IMPERATIVE

—

GERUND

having to

PAST PARTICIPLE

had to

CONDITIONAL

Conditional II

I	would	have to
you	would	have to
he/she/it	would	have to
we	would	have to
you	would	have to
they	would	have to

Conditional Past

I	would have	had to
you	would have	had to
he/she/it	would have	had to
we	would have	had to
you	would have	had to
they	would have	had to

REGULAR

NEED

necessitar, precisar

SIMPLE

Present Simple

I	need
you	need
he/she/it	needs
we	need
you	need
they	need

Past Simple

I	needed
you	needed
he/she/it	needed
we	needed
you	needed
they	needed

Present Perfect

I	have	needed
you	have	needed
he/she/it	has	needed
we	have	needed
you	have	needed
they	have	needed

Past Perfect

I	had	needed
you	had	needed
he/she/it	had	needed
we	had	needed
you	had	needed
they	had	needed

CONTINUOUS

Present Continuous

I	am	needing
you	are	needing
he/she/it	is	needing
we	are	needing
you	are	needing
they	are	needing

Past Continuous

I	was	needing
you	were	needing
he/she/it	was	needing
we	were	needing
you	were	needing
they	were	needing

Present Perfect Continuous

I	have been	needing
you	have been	needing
he/she/it	has been	needing
we	have been	needing
you	have been	needing
they	have been	needing

Past Perfect Continuous

I	had been	needing
you	had been	needing
he/she/it	had been	needing
we	had been	needing
you	had been	needing
they	had been	needing

FUTURE

Future I

I	will	need
you	will	need
he/she/it	will	need
we	will	need
you	will	need
they	will	need

Future I Continuous

I	will be needing
you	will be needing
he/she/it	will be needing
we	will be needing
you	will be needing
they	will be needing

Future II

I	will have	needed
you	will have	needed
he/she/it	will have	needed
we	will have	needed
you	will have	needed
they	will have	needed

Future II Continuous

I	will have been	needing
you	will have been	needing
he/she/it	will have been	needing
we	will have been	needing
you	will have been	needing
they	will have been	needing

IMPERATIVE

—

GERUND

needing

PAST PARTICIPLE

needed

CONDITIONAL

Conditional II

I	would	need
you	would	need
he/she/it	would	need
we	would	need
you	would	need
they	would	need

Conditional Past

I	would have	needed
you	would have	needed
he/she/it	would have	needed
we	would have	needed
you	would have	needed
they	would have	needed

OPEN
abrir

SIMPLE

Present Simple

I	open
you	open
he/she/it	opens
we	open
you	open
they	open

Past Simple

I	opened
you	opened
he/she/it	opened
we	opened
you	opened
they	opened

Present Perfect

I	have	opened
you	have	opened
he/she/it	has	opened
we	have	opened
you	have	opened
they	have	opened

Past Perfect

I	had	opened
you	had	opened
he/she/it	had	opened
we	had	opened
you	had	opened
they	had	opened

CONTINUOUS

Present Continuous

I	am	opening
you	are	opening
he/she/it	is	opening
we	are	opening
you	are	opening
they	are	opening

Past Continuous

I	was	opening
you	were	opening
he/she/it	was	opening
we	were	opening
you	were	opening
they	were	opening

Present Perfect Continuous

I	have been	opening
you	have been	opening
he/she/it	has been	opening
we	have been	opening
you	have been	opening
they	have been	opening

Past Perfect Continuous

I	had been	opening
you	had been	opening
he/she/it	had been	opening
we	had been	opening
you	had been	opening
they	had been	opening

FUTURE

Future I

I	will	open
you	will	open
he/she/it	will	open
we	will	open
you	will	open
they	will	open

Future I Continuous

I	will be opening
you	will be opening
he/she/it	will be opening
we	will be opening
you	will be opening
they	will be opening

Future II

I	will have	opened
you	will have	opened
he/she/it	will have	opened
we	will have	opened
you	will have	opened
they	will have	opened

Future II Continuous

I	will have been	opening
you	will have been	opening
he/she/it	will have been	opening
we	will have been	opening
you	will have been	opening
they	will have been	opening

IMPERATIVE
open

GERUND
opening

PAST PARTICIPLE
opened

CONDITIONAL

Conditional II

I	would	open
you	would	open
he/she/it	would	open
we	would	open
you	would	open
they	would	open

Conditional Past

I	would have	opened
you	would have	opened
he/she/it	would have	opened
we	would have	opened
you	would have	opened
they	would have	opened

IRREGULAR

PAY

pagar

SIMPLE

Present Simple

I	pay
you	pay
he/she/it	pays
we	pay
you	pay
they	pay

Past Simple

I	paid
you	paid
he/she/it	paid
we	paid
you	paid
they	paid

Present Perfect

I	have	paid
you	have	paid
he/she/it	has	paid
we	have	paid
you	have	paid
they	have	paid

Past Perfect

I	had	paid
you	had	paid
he/she/it	had	paid
we	had	paid
you	had	paid
they	had	paid

CONTINUOUS

Present Continuous

I	am	paying
you	are	paying
he/she/it	is	paying
we	are	paying
you	are	paying
they	are	paying

Past Continuous

I	was	paying
you	were	paying
he/she/it	was	paying
we	were	paying
you	were	paying
they	were	paying

Present Perfect Continuous

I	have been	paying
you	have been	paying
he/she/it	has been	paying
we	have been	paying
you	have been	paying
they	have been	paying

Past Perfect Continuous

I	had been	paying
you	had been	paying
he/she/it	had been	paying
we	had been	paying
you	had been	paying
they	had been	paying

FUTURE

Future I

I	will	pay
you	will	pay
he/she/it	will	pay
we	will	pay
you	will	pay
they	will	pay

Future I Continuous

I	will be paying
you	will be paying
he/she/it	will be paying
we	will be paying
you	will be paying
they	will be paying

Future II

I	will have	paid
you	will have	paid
he/she/it	will have	paid
we	will have	paid
you	will have	paid
they	will have	paid

Future II Continuous

I	will have been	paying
you	will have been	paying
he/she/it	will have been	paying
we	will have been	paying
you	will have been	paying
they	will have been	paying

IMPERATIVE

pay

GERUND

paying

PAST PARTICIPLE

paid

CONDITIONAL

Conditional II

I	would	pay
you	would	pay
he/she/it	would	pay
we	would	pay
you	would	pay
they	would	pay

Conditional Past

I	would have	paid
you	would have	paid
he/she/it	would have	paid
we	would have	paid
you	would have	paid
they	would have	paid

PLAY

brincar, jogar, tocar (música)

SIMPLE

Present Simple

I	play
you	play
he/she/it	plays
we	play
you	play
they	play

Past Simple

I	played
you	played
he/she/it	played
we	played
you	played
they	played

Present Perfect

I	have	played
you	have	played
he/she/it	has	played
we	have	played
you	have	played
they	have	played

Past Perfect

I	had	played
you	had	played
he/she/it	had	played
we	had	played
you	had	played
they	had	played

CONTINUOUS

Present Continuous

I	am	playing
you	are	playing
he/she/it	is	playing
we	are	playing
you	are	playing
they	are	playing

Past Continuous

I	was	playing
you	were	playing
he/she/it	was	playing
we	were	playing
you	were	playing
they	were	playing

Present Perfect Continuous

I	have been	playing
you	have been	playing
he/she/it	has been	playing
we	have been	playing
you	have been	playing
they	have been	playing

Past Perfect Continuous

I	had been	playing
you	had been	playing
he/she/it	had been	playing
we	had been	playing
you	had been	playing
they	had been	playing

FUTURE

Future I

I	will	play
you	will	play
he/she/it	will	play
we	will	play
you	will	play
they	will	play

Future I Continuous

I	will be playing
you	will be playing
he/she/it	will be playing
we	will be playing
you	will be playing
they	will be playing

Future II

I	will have	played
you	will have	played
he/she/it	will have	played
we	will have	played
you	will have	played
they	will have	played

Future II Continuous

I	will have been	playing
you	will have been	playing
he/she/it	will have been	playing
we	will have been	playing
you	will have been	playing
they	will have been	playing

IMPERATIVE

play

GERUND

playing

PAST PARTICIPLE

played

CONDITIONAL

Conditional II

I	would	play
you	would	play
he/she/it	would	play
we	would	play
you	would	play
they	would	play

Conditional Past

I	would have	played
you	would have	played
he/she/it	would have	played
we	would have	played
you	would have	played
they	would have	played

IRREGULAR

PUT
pôr

Duplicação de consoante (ver p. 7)

SIMPLE

Present Simple

I	put
you	put
he/she/it	puts
we	put
you	put
they	put

Past Simple

I	**put**
you	**put**
he/she/it	**put**
we	**put**
you	**put**
they	**put**

Present Perfect

I	have	**put**
you	have	**put**
he/she/it	has	**put**
we	have	**put**
you	have	**put**
they	have	**put**

Past Perfect

I	had	**put**
you	had	**put**
he/she/it	had	**put**
we	had	**put**
you	had	**put**
they	had	**put**

CONTINUOUS

Present Continuous

I	am	putting
you	are	putting
he/she/it	is	putting
we	are	putting
you	are	putting
they	are	putting

Past Continuous

I	was	putting
you	were	putting
he/she/it	was	putting
we	were	putting
you	were	putting
they	were	putting

Present Perfect Continuous

I	have been	putting
you	have been	putting
he/she/it	has been	putting
we	have been	putting
you	have been	putting
they	have been	putting

Past Perfect Continuous

I	had been	putting
you	had been	putting
he/she/it	had been	putting
we	had been	putting
you	had been	putting
they	had been	putting

FUTURE

Future I

I	will	put
you	will	put
he/she/it	will	put
we	will	put
you	will	put
they	will	put

Future I Continuous

I	will be putting
you	will be putting
he/she/it	will be putting
we	will be putting
you	will be putting
they	will be putting

Future II

I	will have	**put**
you	will have	**put**
he/she/it	will have	**put**
we	will have	**put**
you	will have	**put**
they	will have	**put**

Future II Continuous

I	will have been	putting
you	will have been	putting
he/she/it	will have been	putting
we	will have been	putting
you	will have been	putting
they	will have been	putting

IMPERATIVE
put

GERUND
putting

PAST PARTICIPLE
put

CONDITIONAL

Conditional II

I	would	put
you	would	put
he/she/it	would	put
we	would	put
you	would	put
they	would	put

Conditional Past

I	would have	**put**
you	would have	**put**
he/she/it	would have	**put**
we	would have	**put**
you	would have	**put**
they	would have	**put**

READ
ler

O *Past Simple* e o *Past Participle* são pronunciados como *red* (vermelho), ou seja, [réd].

SIMPLE

Present Simple

I	read
you	read
he/she/it	reads
we	read
you	read
they	read

Past Simple

I	read
you	read
he/she/it	read
we	read
you	read
they	read

Present Perfect

I	have	read
you	have	read
he/she/it	has	read
we	have	read
you	have	read
they	have	read

Past Perfect

I	had	read
you	had	read
he/she/it	had	read
we	had	read
you	had	read
they	had	read

CONTINUOUS

Present Continuous

I	am	reading
you	are	reading
he/she/it	is	reading
we	are	reading
you	are	reading
they	are	reading

Past Continuous

I	was	reading
you	were	reading
he/she/it	was	reading
we	were	reading
you	were	reading
they	were	reading

Present Perfect Continuous

I	have been	reading
you	have been	reading
he/she/it	has been	reading
we	have been	reading
you	have been	reading
they	have been	reading

Past Perfect Continuous

I	had	been	reading
you	had	been	reading
he/she/it	had	been	reading
we	had	been	reading
you	had	been	reading
they	had	been	reading

FUTURE

Future I

I	will	read
you	will	read
he/she/it	will	read
we	will	read
you	will	read
they	will	read

Future I Continuous

I	will be reading
you	will be reading
he/she/it	will be reading
we	will be reading
you	will be reading
they	will be reading

Future II

I	will have	read
you	will have	read
he/she/it	will have	read
we	will have	read
you	will have	read
they	will have	read

Future II Continuous

I	will have been	reading
you	will have been	reading
he/she/it	will have been	reading
we	will have been	reading
you	will have been	reading
they	will have been	reading

IMPERATIVE
read

GERUND
reading

PAST PARTICIPLE
read

CONDITIONAL

Conditional II

I	would	read
you	would	read
he/she/it	would	read
we	would	read
you	would	read
they	would	read

Conditional Past

I	would have	read
you	would have	read
he/she/it	would have	read
we	would have	read
you	would have	read
they	would have	read

IRREGULAR

RUN

correr

Duplicação de consoante (ver p. 7)

SIMPLE

Present Simple

I	run
you	run
he/she/it	runs
we	run
you	run
they	run

Past Simple

I	ran
you	ran
he/she/it	ran
we	ran
you	ran
they	ran

Present Perfect

I	have	run
you	have	run
he/she/it	has	run
we	have	run
you	have	run
they	have	run

Past Perfect

I	had	run
you	had	run
he/she/it	had	run
we	had	run
you	had	run
they	had	run

CONTINUOUS

Present Continuous

I	am	running
you	are	running
he/she/it	is	running
we	are	running
you	are	running
they	are	running

Past Continuous

I	was	running
you	were	running
he/she/it	was	running
we	were	running
you	were	running
they	were	running

Present Perfect Continuous

I	have	been	running
you	have	been	running
he/she/it	has	been	running
we	have	been	running
you	have	been	running
they	have	been	running

Past Perfect Continuous

I	had	been	running
you	had	been	running
he/she/it	had	been	running
we	had	been	running
you	had	been	running
they	had	been	running

FUTURE

Future I

I	will	run
you	will	run
he/she/it	will	run
we	will	run
you	will	run
they	will	run

Future I Continuous

I	will be running
you	will be running
he/she/it	will be running
we	will be running
you	will be running
they	will be running

Future II

I	will have run
you	will have run
he/she/it	will have run
we	will have run
you	will have run
they	will have run

Future II Continuous

I	will have been	running
you	will have been	running
he/she/it	will have been	running
we	will have been	running
you	will have been	running
they	will have been	running

IMPERATIVE

run

GERUND

running

PAST PARTICIPLE

run

CONDITIONAL

Conditional II

I	would	run
you	would	run
he/she/it	would	run
we	would	run
you	would	run
they	would	run

Conditional Past

I	would have	run
you	would have	run
he/she/it	would have	run
we	would have	run
you	would have	run
they	would have	run

SAY
dizer

A pronúncia de *says* é [séz], afastando-se das demais formas.

SIMPLE

Present Simple

I	say
you	say
he/she/it	says
we	say
you	say
they	say

Past Simple

I	**said**
you	**said**
he/she/it	**said**
we	**said**
you	**said**
they	**said**

Present Perfect

I	have **said**
you	have **said**
he/she/it	has **said**
we	have **said**
you	have **said**
they	have **said**

Past Perfect

I	had **said**
you	had **said**
he/she/it	had **said**
we	had **said**
you	had **said**
they	had **said**

CONTINUOUS

Present Continuous

I	am saying
you	are saying
he/she/it	is saying
we	are saying
you	are saying
they	are saying

Past Continuous

I	was saying
you	were saying
he/she/it	was saying
we	were saying
you	were saying
they	were saying

Present Perfect Continuous

I	have been saying
you	have been saying
he/she/it	has been saying
we	have been saying
you	have been saying
they	have been saying

Past Perfect Continuous

I	had been saying
you	had been saying
he/she/it	had been saying
we	had been saying
you	had been saying
they	had been saying

FUTURE

Future I

I	will say
you	will say
he/she/it	will say
we	will say
you	will say
they	will say

Future I Continuous

I	will be saying
you	will be saying
he/she/it	will be saying
we	will be saying
you	will be saying
they	will be saying

Future II

I	will have **said**
you	will have **said**
he/she/it	will have **said**
we	will have **said**
you	will have **said**
they	will have **said**

Future II Continuous

I	will have been saying
you	will have been saying
he/she/it	will have been saying
we	will have been saying
you	will have been saying
they	will have been saying

IMPERATIVE
say

GERUND
saying

PAST PARTICIPLE
said

CONDITIONAL

Conditional II

I	would say
you	would say
he/she/it	would say
we	would say
you	would say
they	would say

Conditional Past

I	would have **said**
you	would have **said**
he/she/it	would have **said**
we	would have **said**
you	would have **said**
they	would have **said**

SEE
ver

SIMPLE

Present Simple

I	see
you	see
he/she/it	sees
we	see
you	see
they	see

Past Simple

I	**saw**
you	**saw**
he/she/it	**saw**
we	**saw**
you	**saw**
they	**saw**

Present Perfect

I	have	**seen**
you	have	**seen**
he/she/it	has	**seen**
we	have	**seen**
you	have	**seen**
they	have	**seen**

Past Perfect

I	had	**seen**
you	had	**seen**
he/she/it	had	**seen**
we	had	**seen**
you	had	**seen**
they	had	**seen**

CONTINUOUS

Present Continuous

I	am	seeing
you	are	seeing
he/she/it	is	seeing
we	are	seeing
you	are	seeing
they	are	seeing

Past Continuous

I	was	seeing
you	were	seeing
he/she/it	was	seeing
we	were	seeing
you	were	seeing
they	were	seeing

Present Perfect Continuous

I	have been	seeing
you	have been	seeing
he/she/it	has been	seeing
we	have been	seeing
you	have been	seeing
they	have been	seeing

Past Perfect Continuous

I	had been	seeing
you	had been	seeing
he/she/it	had been	seeing
we	had been	seeing
you	had been	seeing
they	had been	seeing

FUTURE

Future I

I	will	see
you	will	see
he/she/it	will	see
we	will	see
you	will	see
they	will	see

Future I Continuous

I	will be seeing
you	will be seeing
he/she/it	will be seeing
we	will be seeing
you	will be seeing
they	will be seeing

Future II

I	will have **seen**
you	will have **seen**
he/she/it	will have **seen**
we	will have **seen**
you	will have **seen**
they	will have **seen**

Future II Continuous

I	will have been	seeing
you	will have been	seeing
he/she/it	will have been	seeing
we	will have been	seeing
you	will have been	seeing
they	will have been	seeing

IMPERATIVE
see

GERUND
seeing

PAST PARTICIPLE
seen

CONDITIONAL

Conditional II

I	would	see
you	would	see
he/she/it	would	see
we	would	see
you	would	see
they	would	see

Conditional Past

I	would have	**seen**
you	would have	**seen**
he/she/it	would have	**seen**
we	would have	**seen**
you	would have	**seen**
they	would have	**seen**

SELL
vender

SIMPLE

Present Simple

I	sell
you	sell
he/she/it	sells
we	sell
you	sell
they	sell

Past Simple

I	sold
you	sold
he/she/it	sold
we	sold
you	sold
they	sold

Present Perfect

I	have	sold
you	have	sold
he/she/it	has	sold
we	have	sold
you	have	sold
they	have	sold

Past Perfect

I	had	sold
you	had	sold
he/she/it	had	sold
we	had	sold
you	had	sold
they	had	sold

CONTINUOUS

Present Continuous

I	am	selling
you	are	selling
he/she/it	is	selling
we	are	selling
you	are	selling
they	are	selling

Past Continuous

I	was	selling
you	were	selling
he/she/it	was	selling
we	were	selling
you	were	selling
they	were	selling

Present Perfect Continuous

I	have been	selling
you	have been	selling
he/she/it	has been	selling
we	have been	selling
you	have been	selling
they	have been	selling

Past Perfect Continuous

I	had been	selling
you	had been	selling
he/she/it	had been	selling
we	had been	selling
you	had been	selling
they	had been	selling

FUTURE

Future I

I	will	sell
you	will	sell
he/she/it	will	sell
we	will	sell
you	will	sell
they	will	sell

Future I Continuous

I	will be selling
you	will be selling
he/she/it	will be selling
we	will be selling
you	will be selling
they	will be selling

Future II

I	will have	sold
you	will have	sold
he/she/it	will have	sold
we	will have	sold
you	will have	sold
they	will have	sold

Future II Continuous

I	will have been	selling
you	will have been	selling
he/she/it	will have been	selling
we	will have been	selling
you	will have been	selling
they	will have been	selling

IMPERATIVE
sell

GERUND
selling

PAST PARTICIPLE
sold

CONDITIONAL

Conditional II

I	would	sell
you	would	sell
he/she/it	would	sell
we	would	sell
you	would	sell
they	would	sell

Conditional Past

I	would have	sold
you	would have	sold
he/she/it	would have	sold
we	would have	sold
you	would have	sold
they	would have	sold

IRREGULAR

SEND
enviar

SIMPLE

Present Simple

I	send
you	send
he/she/it	sends
we	send
you	send
they	send

Past Simple

I	sent
you	sent
he/she/it	sent
we	sent
you	sent
they	sent

Present Perfect

I	have	sent
you	have	sent
he/she/it	has	sent
we	have	sent
you	have	sent
they	have	sent

Past Perfect

I	had	sent
you	had	sent
he/she/it	had	sent
we	had	sent
you	had	sent
they	had	sent

CONTINUOUS

Present Continuous

I	am	sending
you	are	sending
he/she/it	is	sending
we	are	sending
you	are	sending
they	are	sending

Past Continuous

I	was	sending
you	were	sending
he/she/it	was	sending
we	were	sending
you	were	sending
they	were	sending

Present Perfect Continuous

I	have been	sending
you	have been	sending
he/she/it	has been	sending
we	have been	sending
you	have been	sending
they	have been	sending

Past Perfect Continuous

I	had	been	sending
you	had	been	sending
he/she/it	had	been	sending
we	had	been	sending
you	had	been	sending
they	had	been	sending

FUTURE

Future I

I	will	send
you	will	send
he/she/it	will	send
we	will	send
you	will	send
they	will	send

Future I Continuous

I	will be sending
you	will be sending
he/she/it	will be sending
we	will be sending
you	will be sending
they	will be sending

Future II

I	will have	sent
you	will have	sent
he/she/it	will have	sent
we	will have	sent
you	will have	sent
they	will have	sent

Future II Continuous

I	will have been	sending
you	will have been	sending
he/she/it	will have been	sending
we	will have been	sending
you	will have been	sending
they	will have been	sending

IMPERATIVE
send

GERUND
sending

PAST PARTICIPLE
sent

CONDITIONAL

Conditional II

I	would	send
you	would	send
he/she/it	would	send
we	would	send
you	would	send
they	would	send

Conditional Past

I	would have	sent
you	would have	sent
he/she/it	would have	sent
we	would have	sent
you	would have	sent
they	would have	sent

SHUT
fechar

Duplicação de consoante (ver p. 7)

SIMPLE

Present Simple

I	shut
you	shut
he/she/it	shuts
we	shut
you	shut
they	shut

Past Simple

I	shut
you	shut
he/she/it	shut
we	shut
you	shut
they	shut

Present Perfect

I	have shut
you	have shut
he/she/it	has shut
we	have shut
you	have shut
they	have shut

Past Perfect

I	had shut
you	had shut
he/she/it	had shut
we	had shut
you	had shut
they	had shut

CONTINUOUS

Present Continuous

I	am shutting
you	are shutting
he/she/it	is shutting
we	are shutting
you	are shutting
they	are shutting

Past Continuous

I	was shutting
you	were shutting
he/she/it	was shutting
we	were shutting
you	were shutting
they	were shutting

Present Perfect Continuous

I	have been shutting
you	have been shutting
he/she/it	has been shutting
we	have been shutting
you	have been shutting
they	have been shutting

Past Perfect Continuous

I	had been shutting
you	had been shutting
he/she/it	had been shutting
we	had been shutting
you	had been shutting
they	had been shutting

FUTURE

Future I

I	will shut
you	will shut
he/she/it	will shut
we	will shut
you	will shut
they	will shut

Future I Continuous

I	will be shutting
you	will be shutting
he/she/it	will be shutting
we	will be shutting
you	will be shutting
they	will be shutting

Future II

I	will have shut
you	will have shut
he/she/it	will have shut
we	will have shut
you	will have shut
they	will have shut

Future II Continuous

I	will have been shutting
you	will have been shutting
he/she/it	will have been shutting
we	will have been shutting
you	will have been shutting
they	will have been shutting

IMPERATIVE
shut

GERUND
shutting

PAST PARTICIPLE
shut

CONDITIONAL

Conditional II

I	would shut
you	would shut
he/she/it	would shut
we	would shut
you	would shut
they	would shut

Conditional Past

I	would have shut
you	would have shut
he/she/it	would have shut
we	would have shut
you	would have shut
they	would have shut

SIT
sentar

Duplicação de consoante (ver p. 7)

SIMPLE

Present Simple

I	sit
you	sit
he/she/it	sits
we	sit
you	sit
they	sit

Past Simple

I	**sat**
you	**sat**
he/she/it	**sat**
we	**sat**
you	**sat**
they	**sat**

Present Perfect

I	have	**sat**
you	have	**sat**
he/she/it	has	**sat**
we	have	**sat**
you	have	**sat**
they	have	**sat**

Past Perfect

I	had	**sat**
you	had	**sat**
he/she/it	had	**sat**
we	had	**sat**
you	had	**sat**
they	had	**sat**

CONTINUOUS

Present Continuous

I	am	sitting
you	are	sitting
he/she/it	is	sitting
we	are	sitting
you	are	sitting
they	are	sitting

Past Continuous

I	was	sitting
you	were	sitting
he/she/it	was	sitting
we	were	sitting
you	were	sitting
they	were	sitting

Present Perfect Continuous

I	have been	sitting
you	have been	sitting
he/she/it	has been	sitting
we	have been	sitting
you	have been	sitting
they	have been	sitting

Past Perfect Continuous

I	had been	sitting
you	had been	sitting
he/she/it	had been	sitting
we	had been	sitting
you	had been	sitting
they	had been	sitting

FUTURE

Future I

I	will	sit
you	will	sit
he/she/it	will	sit
we	will	sit
you	will	sit
they	will	sit

Future I Continuous

I	will be sitting
you	will be sitting
he/she/it	will be sitting
we	will be sitting
you	will be sitting
they	will be sitting

Future II

I	will have	**sat**
you	will have	**sat**
he/she/it	will have	**sat**
we	will have	**sat**
you	will have	**sat**
they	will have	**sat**

Future II Continuous

I	will have been	sitting
you	will have been	sitting
he/she/it	will have been	sitting
we	will have been	sitting
you	will have been	sitting
they	will have been	sitting

IMPERATIVE
sit

GERUND
sitting

PAST PARTICIPLE
sat

CONDITIONAL

Conditional II

I	would	sit
you	would	sit
he/she/it	would	sit
we	would	sit
you	would	sit
they	would	sit

Conditional Past

I	would have	**sat**
you	would have	**sat**
he/she/it	would have	**sat**
we	would have	**sat**
you	would have	**sat**
they	would have	**sat**

SLEEP
dormir

SIMPLE

Present Simple

I	sleep
you	sleep
he/she/it	sleeps
we	sleep
you	sleep
they	sleep

Past Simple

I	slept
you	slept
he/she/it	slept
we	slept
you	slept
they	slept

Present Perfect

I	have	slept
you	have	slept
he/she/it	has	slept
we	have	slept
you	have	slept
they	have	slept

Past Perfect

I	had	slept
you	had	slept
he/she/it	had	slept
we	had	slept
you	had	slept
they	had	slept

CONTINUOUS

Present Continuous

I	am	sleeping
you	are	sleeping
he/she/it	is	sleeping
we	are	sleeping
you	are	sleeping
they	are	sleeping

Past Continuous

I	was	sleeping
you	were	sleeping
he/she/it	was	sleeping
we	were	sleeping
you	were	sleeping
they	were	sleeping

Present Perfect Continuous

I	have been	sleeping
you	have been	sleeping
he/she/it	has been	sleeping
we	have been	sleeping
you	have been	sleeping
they	have been	sleeping

Past Perfect Continuous

I	had been	sleeping
you	had been	sleeping
he/she/it	had been	sleeping
we	had been	sleeping
you	had been	sleeping
they	had been	sleeping

FUTURE

Future I

I	will	sleep
you	will	sleep
he/she/it	will	sleep
we	will	sleep
you	will	sleep
they	will	sleep

Future I Continuous

I	will be sleeping
you	will be sleeping
he/she/it	will be sleeping
we	will be sleeping
you	will be sleeping
they	will be sleeping

Future II

I	will have	slept
you	will have	slept
he/she/it	will have	slept
we	will have	slept
you	will have	slept
they	will have	slept

Future II Continuous

I	will have been	sleeping
you	will have been	sleeping
he/she/it	will have been	sleeping
we	will have been	sleeping
you	will have been	sleeping
they	will have been	sleeping

IMPERATIVE
sleep

GERUND
sleeping

PAST PARTICIPLE
slept

CONDITIONAL

Conditional II

I	would	sleep
you	would	sleep
he/she/it	would	sleep
we	would	sleep
you	would	sleep
they	would	sleep

Conditional Past

I	would have	slept
you	would have	slept
he/she/it	would have	slept
we	would have	slept
you	would have	slept
they	would have	slept

SPEAK
falar

SIMPLE

Present Simple

I	speak
you	speak
he/she/it	speaks
we	speak
you	speak
they	speak

Past Simple

I	spoke
you	spoke
he/she/it	spoke
we	spoke
you	spoke
they	spoke

Present Perfect

I	have	spoken
you	have	spoken
he/she/it	has	spoken
we	have	spoken
you	have	spoken
they	have	spoken

Past Perfect

I	had	spoken
you	had	spoken
he/she/it	had	spoken
we	had	spoken
you	had	spoken
they	had	spoken

CONTINUOUS

Present Continuous

I	am	speaking
you	are	speaking
he/she/it	is	speaking
we	are	speaking
you	are	speaking
they	are	speaking

Past Continuous

I	was	speaking
you	were	speaking
he/she/it	was	speaking
we	were	speaking
you	were	speaking
they	were	speaking

Present Perfect Continuous

I	have been	speaking
you	have been	speaking
he/she/it	has been	speaking
we	have been	speaking
you	have been	speaking
they	have been	speaking

Past Perfect Continuous

I	had been	speaking
you	had been	speaking
he/she/it	had been	speaking
we	had been	speaking
you	had been	speaking
they	had been	speaking

FUTURE

Future I

I	will	speak
you	will	speak
he/she/it	will	speak
we	will	speak
you	will	speak
they	will	speak

Future I Continuous

I	will be speaking
you	will be speaking
he/she/it	will be speaking
we	will be speaking
you	will be speaking
they	will be speaking

Future II

I	will have	spoken
you	will have	spoken
he/she/it	will have	spoken
we	will have	spoken
you	will have	spoken
they	will have	spoken

Future II Continuous

I	will have been	speaking
you	will have been	speaking
he/she/it	will have been	speaking
we	will have been	speaking
you	will have been	speaking
they	will have been	speaking

IMPERATIVE
speak

GERUND
speaking

PAST PARTICIPLE
spoken

CONDITIONAL

Conditional II

I	would	speak
you	would	speak
he/she/it	would	speak
we	would	speak
you	would	speak
they	would	speak

Conditional Past

I	would have	spoken
you	would have	spoken
he/she/it	would have	spoken
we	would have	spoken
you	would have	spoken
they	would have	spoken

SPEND
despender

SIMPLE

Present Simple

I	spend
you	spend
he/she/it	spends
we	spend
you	spend
they	spend

Past Simple

I	spent
you	spent
he/she/it	spent
we	spent
you	spent
they	spent

Present Perfect

I	have	spent
you	have	spent
he/she/it	has	spent
we	have	spent
you	have	spent
they	have	spent

Past Perfect

I	had	spent
you	had	spent
he/she/it	had	spent
we	had	spent
you	had	spent
they	had	spent

CONTINUOUS

Present Continuous

I	am	spending
you	are	spending
he/she/it	is	spending
we	are	spending
you	are	spending
they	are	spending

Past Continuous

I	was	spending
you	were	spending
he/she/it	was	spending
we	were	spending
you	were	spending
they	were	spending

Present Perfect Continuous

I	have been	spending
you	have been	spending
he/she/it	has been	spending
we	have been	spending
you	have been	spending
they	have been	spending

Past Perfect Continuous

I	had been	spending
you	had been	spending
he/she/it	had been	spending
we	had been	spending
you	had been	spending
they	had been	spending

FUTURE

Future I

I	will	spend
you	will	spend
he/she/it	will	spend
we	will	spend
you	will	spend
they	will	spend

Future I Continuous

I	will be spending
you	will be spending
he/she/it	will be spending
we	will be spending
you	will be spending
they	will be spending

Future II

I	will have	spent
you	will have	spent
he/she/it	will have	spent
we	will have	spent
you	will have	spent
they	will have	spent

Future II Continuous

I	will have been	spending
you	will have been	spending
he/she/it	will have been	spending
we	will have been	spending
you	will have been	spending
they	will have been	spending

IMPERATIVE
spend

GERUND
spending

PAST PARTICIPLE
spent

CONDITIONAL

Conditional II

I	would	spend
you	would	spend
he/she/it	would	spend
we	would	spend
you	would	spend
they	would	spend

Conditional Past

I	would have	spent
you	would have	spent
he/she/it	would have	spent
we	would have	spent
you	would have	spent
they	would have	spent

STAND
ficar em pé

SIMPLE

Present Simple

I	stand
you	stand
he/she/it	stands
we	stand
you	stand
they	stand

Past Simple

I	stood
you	stood
he/she/it	stood
we	stood
you	stood
they	stood

Present Perfect

I	have	stood
you	have	stood
he/she/it	has	stood
we	have	stood
you	have	stood
they	have	stood

Past Perfect

I	had	stood
you	had	stood
he/she/it	had	stood
we	had	stood
you	had	stood
they	had	stood

CONTINUOUS

Present Continuous

I	am	standing
you	are	standing
he/she/it	is	standing
we	are	standing
you	are	standing
they	are	standing

Past Continuous

I	was	standing
you	were	standing
he/she/it	was	standing
we	were	standing
you	were	standing
they	were	standing

Present Perfect Continuous

I	have been	standing
you	have been	standing
he/she/it	has been	standing
we	have been	standing
you	have been	standing
they	have been	standing

Past Perfect Continuous

I	had been	standing
you	had been	standing
he/she/it	had been	standing
we	had been	standing
you	had been	standing
they	had been	standing

FUTURE

Future I

I	will	stand
you	will	stand
he/she/it	will	stand
we	will	stand
you	will	stand
they	will	stand

Future I Continuous

I	will be standing
you	will be standing
he/she/it	will be standing
we	will be standing
you	will be standing
they	will be standing

Future II

I	will have	stood
you	will have	stood
he/she/it	will have	stood
we	will have	stood
you	will have	stood
they	will have	stood

Future II Continuous

I	will have been	standing
you	will have been	standing
he/she/it	will have been	standing
we	will have been	standing
you	will have been	standing
they	will have been	standing

IMPERATIVE
stand

GERUND
standing

PAST PARTICIPLE
stood

CONDITIONAL

Conditional II

I	would	stand
you	would	stand
he/she/it	would	stand
we	would	stand
you	would	stand
they	would	stand

Conditional Past

I	would have	stood
you	would have	stood
he/she/it	would have	stood
we	would have	stood
you	would have	stood
they	would have	stood

STAY
permanecer

SIMPLE

Present Simple

I	stay
you	stay
he/she/it	stays
we	stay
you	stay
they	stay

Past Simple

I	stayed
you	stayed
he/she/it	stayed
we	stayed
you	stayed
they	stayed

Present Perfect

I	have	stayed
you	have	stayed
he/she/it	has	stayed
we	have	stayed
you	have	stayed
they	have	stayed

Past Perfect

I	had	stayed
you	had	stayed
he/she/it	had	stayed
we	had	stayed
you	had	stayed
they	had	stayed

CONTINUOUS

Present Continuous

I	am	staying
you	are	staying
he/she/it	is	staying
we	are	staying
you	are	staying
they	are	staying

Past Continuous

I	was	staying
you	were	staying
he/she/it	was	staying
we	were	staying
you	were	staying
they	were	staying

Present Perfect Continuous

I	have been	staying
you	have been	staying
he/she/it	has been	staying
we	have been	staying
you	have been	staying
they	have been	staying

Past Perfect Continuous

I	had been	staying
you	had been	staying
he/she/it	had been	staying
we	had been	staying
you	had been	staying
they	had been	staying

FUTURE

Future I

I	will	stay
you	will	stay
he/she/it	will	stay
we	will	stay
you	will	stay
they	will	stay

Future I Continuous

I	will be staying
you	will be staying
he/she/it	will be staying
we	will be staying
you	will be staying
they	will be staying

Future II

I	will have stayed
you	will have stayed
he/she/it	will have stayed
we	will have stayed
you	will have stayed
they	will have stayed

Future II Continuous

I	will have been	staying
you	will have been	staying
he/she/it	will have been	staying
we	will have been	staying
you	will have been	staying
they	will have been	staying

IMPERATIVE
stay

GERUND
staying

PAST PARTICIPLE
stayed

CONDITIONAL

Conditional II

I	would	stay
you	would	stay
he/she/it	would	stay
we	would	stay
you	would	stay
they	would	stay

Conditional Past

I	would have	stayed
you	would have	stayed
he/she/it	would have	stayed
we	would have	stayed
you	would have	stayed
they	would have	stayed

SWIM
nadar

Duplicação de consoante (ver p. 7)

SIMPLE

Present Simple

I	swim
you	swim
he/she/it	swims
we	swim
you	swim
they	swim

Past Simple

I	swam
you	swam
he/she/it	swam
we	swam
you	swam
they	swam

Present Perfect

I	have	swum
you	have	swum
he/she/it	has	swum
we	have	swum
you	have	swum
they	have	swum

Past Perfect

I	had	swum
you	had	swum
he/she/it	had	swum
we	had	swum
you	had	swum
they	had	swum

CONTINUOUS

Present Continuous

I	am	swimming
you	are	swimming
he/she/it	is	swimming
we	are	swimming
you	are	swimming
they	are	swimming

Past Continuous

I	was	swimming
you	were	swimming
he/she/it	was	swimming
we	were	swimming
you	were	swimming
they	were	swimming

Present Perfect Continuous

I	have been	swimming
you	have been	swimming
he/she/it	has been	swimming
we	have been	swimming
you	have been	swimming
they	have been	swimming

Past Perfect Continuous

I	had been	swimming
you	had been	swimming
he/she/it	had been	swimming
we	had been	swimming
you	had been	swimming
they	had been	swimming

FUTURE

Future I

I	will	swim
you	will	swim
he/she/it	will	swim
we	will	swim
you	will	swim
they	will	swim

Future I Continuous

I	will be swimming
you	will be swimming
he/she/it	will be swimming
we	will be swimming
you	will be swimming
they	will be swimming

Future II

I	will have swum
you	will have swum
he/she/it	will have swum
we	will have swum
you	will have swum
they	will have swum

Future II Continuous

I	will have been swimming
you	will have been swimming
he/she/it	will have been swimming
we	will have been swimming
you	will have been swimming
they	will have been swimming

IMPERATIVE
swim

GERUND
swimming

PAST PARTICIPLE
swum

CONDITIONAL

Conditional II

I	would	swim
you	would	swim
he/she/it	would	swim
we	would	swim
you	would	swim
they	would	swim

Conditional Past

I	would have swum
you	would have swum
he/she/it	would have swum
we	would have swum
you	would have swum
they	would have swum

TAKE

pegar, tomar

+ *-ing* → ~~e~~ (ver p. 8)

SIMPLE

Present Simple

I	take
you	take
he/she/it	takes
we	take
you	take
they	take

Past Simple

I	took
you	took
he/she/it	took
we	took
you	took
they	took

Present Perfect

I	have	taken
you	have	taken
he/she/it	has	taken
we	have	taken
you	have	taken
they	have	taken

Past Perfect

I	had	taken
you	had	taken
he/she/it	had	taken
we	had	taken
you	had	taken
they	had	taken

CONTINUOUS

Present Continuous

I	am	taking
you	are	taking
he/she/it	is	taking
we	are	taking
you	are	taking
they	are	taking

Past Continuous

I	was	taking
you	were	taking
he/she/it	was	taking
we	were	taking
you	were	taking
they	were	taking

Present Perfect Continuous

I	have been	taking
you	have been	taking
he/she/it	has been	taking
we	have been	taking
you	have been	taking
they	have been	taking

Past Perfect Continuous

I	had been	taking
you	had been	taking
he/she/it	had been	taking
we	had been	taking
you	had been	taking
they	had been	taking

FUTURE

Future I

I	will	take
you	will	take
he/she/it	will	take
we	will	take
you	will	take
they	will	take

Future I Continuous

I	will be taking
you	will be taking
he/she/it	will be taking
we	will be taking
you	will be taking
they	will be taking

Future II

I	will have taken
you	will have taken
he/she/it	will have taken
we	will have taken
you	will have taken
they	will have taken

Future II Continuous

I	will have been	taking
you	will have been	taking
he/she/it	will have been	taking
we	will have been	taking
you	will have been	taking
they	will have been	taking

IMPERATIVE

take

GERUND

taking

PAST PARTICIPLE

taken

CONDITIONAL

Conditional II

I	would	take
you	would	take
he/she/it	would	take
we	would	take
you	would	take
they	would	take

Conditional Past

I	would have	taken
you	would have	taken
he/she/it	would have	taken
we	would have	taken
you	would have	taken
they	would have	taken

IRREGULAR

THINK
pensar

SIMPLE

Present Simple

I	think
you	think
he/she/it	thinks
we	think
you	think
they	think

Past Simple

I	thought
you	thought
he/she/it	thought
we	thought
you	thought
they	thought

Present Perfect

I	have	thought
you	have	thought
he/she/it	has	thought
we	have	thought
you	have	thought
they	have	thought

Past Perfect

I	had	thought
you	had	thought
he/she/it	had	thought
we	had	thought
you	had	thought
they	had	thought

CONTINUOUS

Present Continuous

I	am	thinking
you	are	thinking
he/she/it	is	thinking
we	are	thinking
you	are	thinking
they	are	thinking

Past Continuous

I	was	thinking
you	were	thinking
he/she/it	was	thinking
we	were	thinking
you	were	thinking
they	were	thinking

Present Perfect Continuous

I	have been	thinking
you	have been	thinking
he/she/it	has been	thinking
we	have been	thinking
you	have been	thinking
they	have been	thinking

Past Perfect Continuous

I	had been	thinking
you	had been	thinking
he/she/it	had been	thinking
we	had been	thinking
you	had been	thinking
they	had been	thinking

FUTURE

Future I

I	will	think
you	will	think
he/she/it	will	think
we	will	think
you	will	think
they	will	think

Future I Continuous

I	will be thinking
you	will be thinking
he/she/it	will be thinking
we	will be thinking
you	will be thinking
they	will be thinking

Future II

I	will have	thought
you	will have	thought
he/she/it	will have	thought
we	will have	thought
you	will have	thought
they	will have	thought

Future II Continuous

I	will have been	thinking
you	will have been	thinking
he/she/it	will have been	thinking
we	will have been	thinking
you	will have been	thinking
they	will have been	thinking

IMPERATIVE
think

GERUND
thinking

PAST PARTICIPLE
thought

CONDITIONAL

Conditional II

I	would	think
you	would	think
he/she/it	would	think
we	would	think
you	would	think
they	would	think

Conditional Past

I	would have	thought
you	would have	thought
he/she/it	would have	thought
we	would have	thought
you	would have	thought
they	would have	thought

TRAVEL
viajar

Duplicação de consoante no IB (ver p. 7), não no IA.

SIMPLE

Present Simple

I	travel
you	travel
he/she/it	travels
we	travel
you	travel
they	travel

Past Simple

I	travelled
you	travelled
he/she/it	travelled
we	travelled
you	travelled
they	travelled

Present Perfect

I	have	travelled
you	have	travelled
he/she/it	has	travelled
we	have	travelled
you	have	travelled
they	have	travelled

Past Perfect

I	had	travelled
you	had	travelled
he/she/it	had	travelled
we	had	travelled
you	had	travelled
they	had	travelled

CONTINUOUS

Present Continuous

I	am	travelling
you	are	travelling
he/she/it	is	travelling
we	are	travelling
you	are	travelling
they	are	travelling

Past Continuous

I	was	travelling
you	were	travelling
he/she/it	was	travelling
we	were	travelling
you	were	travelling
they	were	travelling

Present Perfect Continuous

I	have been	travelling
you	have been	travelling
he/she/it	has been	travelling
we	have been	travelling
you	have been	travelling
they	have been	travelling

Past Perfect Continuous

I	had	been	travelling
you	had	been	travelling
he/she/it	had	been	travelling
we	had	been	travelling
you	had	been	travelling
they	had	been	travelling

FUTURE

Future I

I	will	travel
you	will	travel
he/she/it	will	travel
we	will	travel
you	will	travel
they	will	travel

Future I Continuous

I	will be travelling
you	will be travelling
he/she/it	will be travelling
we	will be travelling
you	will be travelling
they	will be travelling

Future II

I	will have	travelled
you	will have	travelled
he/she/it	will have	travelled
we	will have	travelled
you	will have	travelled
they	will have	travelled

Future II Continuous

I	will have been	travelling
you	will have been	travelling
he/she/it	will have been	travelling
we	will have been	travelling
you	will have been	travelling
they	will have been	travelling

IMPERATIVE
travel

GERUND
travelling

PAST PARTICIPLE
travelled

CONDITIONAL

Conditional II

I	would	travel
you	would	travel
he/she/it	would	travel
we	would	travel
you	would	travel
they	would	travel

Conditional Past

I	would have	travelled
you	would have	travelled
he/she/it	would have	travelled
we	would have	travelled
you	would have	travelled
they	would have	travelled

VISIT
visitar

SIMPLE

Present Simple

I	visit
you	visit
he/she/it	visits
we	visit
you	visit
they	visit

Past Simple

I	visited
you	visited
he/she/it	visited
we	visited
you	visited
they	visited

Present Perfect

I	have	visited
you	have	visited
he/she/it	has	visited
we	have	visited
you	have	visited
they	have	visited

Past Perfect

I	had	visited
you	had	visited
he/she/it	had	visited
we	had	visited
you	had	visited
they	had	visited

CONTINUOUS

Present Continuous

I	am	visiting
you	are	visiting
he/she/it	is	visiting
we	are	visiting
you	are	visiting
they	are	visiting

Past Continuous

I	was	visiting
you	were	visiting
he/she/it	was	visiting
we	were	visiting
you	were	visiting
they	were	visiting

Present Perfect Continuous

I	have been	visiting
you	have been	visiting
he/she/it	has been	visiting
we	have been	visiting
you	have been	visiting
they	have been	visiting

Past Perfect Continuous

I	had been	visiting
you	had been	visiting
he/she/it	had been	visiting
we	had been	visiting
you	had been	visiting
they	had been	visiting

FUTURE

Future I

I	will	visit
you	will	visit
he/she/it	will	visit
we	will	visit
you	will	visit
they	will	visit

Future I Continuous

I	will be visiting
you	will be visiting
he/she/it	will be visiting
we	will be visiting
you	will be visiting
they	will be visiting

Future II

I	will have	visited
you	will have	visited
he/she/it	will have	visited
we	will have	visited
you	will have	visited
they	will have	visited

Future II Continuous

I	will have been	visiting
you	will have been	visiting
he/she/it	will have been	visiting
we	will have been	visiting
you	will have been	visiting
they	will have been	visiting

IMPERATIVE
visit

GERUND
visiting

PAST PARTICIPLE
visited

CONDITIONAL

Conditional II

I	would	visit
you	would	visit
he/she/it	would	visit
we	would	visit
you	would	visit
they	would	visit

Conditional Past

I	would have	visited
you	would have	visited
he/she/it	would have	visited
we	would have	visited
you	would have	visited
they	would have	visited

WAIT
esperar

SIMPLE

Present Simple

I	wait
you	wait
he/she/it	waits
we	wait
you	wait
they	wait

Past Simple

I	waited
you	waited
he/she/it	waited
we	waited
you	waited
they	waited

Present Perfect

I	have	waited
you	have	waited
he/she/it	has	waited
we	have	waited
you	have	waited
they	have	waited

Past Perfect

I	had	waited
you	had	waited
he/she/it	had	waited
we	had	waited
you	had	waited
they	had	waited

CONTINUOUS

Present Continuous

I	am	waiting
you	are	waiting
he/she/it	is	waiting
we	are	waiting
you	are	waiting
they	are	waiting

Past Continuous

I	was	waiting
you	were	waiting
he/she/it	was	waiting
we	were	waiting
you	were	waiting
they	were	waiting

Present Perfect Continuous

I	have been	waiting
you	have been	waiting
he/she/it	has been	waiting
we	have been	waiting
you	have been	waiting
they	have been	waiting

Past Perfect Continuous

I	had been	waiting
you	had been	waiting
he/she/it	had been	waiting
we	had been	waiting
you	had been	waiting
they	had been	waiting

FUTURE

Future I

I	will	wait
you	will	wait
he/she/it	will	wait
we	will	wait
you	will	wait
they	will	wait

Future I Continuous

I	will be waiting
you	will be waiting
he/she/it	will be waiting
we	will be waiting
you	will be waiting
they	will be waiting

Future II

I	will have	waited
you	will have	waited
he/she/it	will have	waited
we	will have	waited
you	will have	waited
they	will have	waited

Future II Continuous

I	will have been	waiting
you	will have been	waiting
he/she/it	will have been	waiting
we	will have been	waiting
you	will have been	waiting
they	will have been	waiting

IMPERATIVE
wait

GERUND
waiting

PAST PARTICIPLE
waited

CONDITIONAL

Conditional II

I	would	wait
you	would	wait
he/she/it	would	wait
we	would	wait
you	would	wait
they	would	wait

Conditional Past

I	would have	waited
you	would have	waited
he/she/it	would have	waited
we	would have	waited
you	would have	waited
they	would have	waited

REGULAR
VERBO MODAL

WANT
querer

Não há *Present Continuous*.

SIMPLE

Present Simple

I	want
you	want
he/she/it	wants
we	want
you	want
they	want

Past Simple

I	wanted
you	wanted
he/she/it	wanted
we	wanted
you	wanted
they	wanted

Present Perfect

I	have	wanted
you	have	wanted
he/she/it	has	wanted
we	have	wanted
you	have	wanted
they	have	wanted

Past Perfect

I	had	wanted
you	had	wanted
he/she/it	had	wanted
we	had	wanted
you	had	wanted
they	had	wanted

CONTINUOUS

Present Continuous

—

Past Continuous*

I	was	wanting
you	were	wanting
he/she/it	was	wanting
we	were	wanting
you	were	wanting
they	were	wanting

Present Perfect Continuous

I	have	been	wanting
you	have	been	wanting
he/she/it	has	been	wanting
we	have	been	wanting
you	have	been	wanting
they	have	been	wanting

Past Perfect Continuous

I	had	been	wanting
you	had	been	wanting
he/she/it	had	been	wanting
we	had	been	wanting
you	had	been	wanting
they	had	been	wanting

FUTURE

Future I

I	will	want
you	will	want
he/she/it	will	want
we	will	want
you	will	want
they	will	want

Future I Continuous

I	will be wanting
you	will be wanting
he/she/it	will be wanting
we	will be wanting
you	will be wanting
they	will be wanting

Future II

I	will have	wanted
you	will have	wanted
he/she/it	will have	wanted
we	will have	wanted
you	will have	wanted
they	will have	wanted

Future II Continuous

I	will have been	wanting
you	will have been	wanting
he/she/it	will have been	wanting
we	will have been	wanting
you	will have been	wanting
they	will have been	wanting

IMPERATIVE
want*

GERUND
wanting

PAST PARTICIPLE
wanted

CONDITIONAL

Conditional II

I	would	want
you	would	want
he/she/it	would	want
we	would	want
you	would	want
they	would	want

Conditional Past

I	would have	wanted
you	would have	wanted
he/she/it	would have	wanted
we	would have	wanted
you	would have	wanted
they	would have	wanted

* raro

WASH
lavar

+ ***-es*** na 3ª pessoa do singular do *Present Simple* (ver p. 7; pronúncia, ver p. 8)

SIMPLE

Present Simple

I	wash
you	wash
he/she/it	washes
we	wash
you	wash
they	wash

Past Simple

I	washed
you	washed
he/she/it	washed
we	washed
you	washed
they	washed

Present Perfect

I	have	washed
you	have	washed
he/she/it	has	washed
we	have	washed
you	have	washed
they	have	washed

Past Perfect

I	had	washed
you	had	washed
he/she/it	had	washed
we	had	washed
you	had	washed
they	had	washed

CONTINUOUS

Present Continuous

I	am	washing
you	are	washing
he/she/it	is	washing
we	are	washing
you	are	washing
they	are	washing

Past Continuous

I	was	washing
you	were	washing
he/she/it	was	washing
we	were	washing
you	were	washing
they	were	washing

Present Perfect Continuous

I	have been	washing
you	have been	washing
he/she/it	has been	washing
we	have been	washing
you	have been	washing
they	have been	washing

Past Perfect Continuous

I	had been	washing
you	had been	washing
he/she/it	had been	washing
we	had been	washing
you	had been	washing
they	had been	washing

FUTURE

Future I

I	will	wash
you	will	wash
he/she/it	will	wash
we	will	wash
you	will	wash
they	will	wash

Future I Continuous

I	will be washing
you	will be washing
he/she/it	will be washing
we	will be washing
you	will be washing
they	will be washing

Future II

I	will have	washed
you	will have	washed
he/she/it	will have	washed
we	will have	washed
you	will have	washed
they	will have	washed

Future II Continuous

I	will have been	washing
you	will have been	washing
he/she/it	will have been	washing
we	will have been	washing
you	will have been	washing
they	will have been	washing

IMPERATIVE
wash

GERUND
washing

PAST PARTICIPLE
washed

CONDITIONAL

Conditional II

I	would	wash
you	would	wash
he/she/it	would	wash
we	would	wash
you	would	wash
they	would	wash

Conditional Past

I	would have	washed
you	would have	washed
he/she/it	would have	washed
we	would have	washed
you	would have	washed
they	would have	washed

IRREGULAR

WEAR
vestir

SIMPLE

Present Simple

I	wear
you	wear
he/she/it	wears
we	wear
you	wear
they	wear

Past Simple

I	wore
you	wore
he/she/it	wore
we	wore
you	wore
they	wore

Present Perfect

I	have	worn
you	have	worn
he/she/it	has	worn
we	have	worn
you	have	worn
they	have	worn

Past Perfect

I	had	worn
you	had	worn
he/she/it	had	worn
we	had	worn
you	had	worn
they	had	worn

CONTINUOUS

Present Continuous

I	am	wearing
you	are	wearing
he/she/it	is	wearing
we	are	wearing
you	are	wearing
they	are	wearing

Past Continuous

I	was	wearing
you	were	wearing
he/she/it	was	wearing
we	were	wearing
you	were	wearing
they	were	wearing

Present Perfect Continuous

I	have been	wearing
you	have been	wearing
he/she/it	has been	wearing
we	have been	wearing
you	have been	wearing
they	have been	wearing

Past Perfect Continuous

I	had	been	wearing
you	had	been	wearing
he/she/it	had	been	wearing
we	had	been	wearing
you	had	been	wearing
they	had	been	wearing

FUTURE

Future I

I	will	wear
you	will	wear
he/she/it	will	wear
we	will	wear
you	will	wear
they	will	wear

Future I Continuous

I	will be wearing
you	will be wearing
he/she/it	will be wearing
we	will be wearing
you	will be wearing
they	will be wearing

Future II

I	will have	worn
you	will have	worn
he/she/it	will have	worn
we	will have	worn
you	will have	worn
they	will have	worn

Future II Continuous

I	will have been	wearing
you	will have been	wearing
he/she/it	will have been	wearing
we	will have been	wearing
you	will have been	wearing
they	will have been	wearing

IMPERATIVE
wear

GERUND
wearing

PAST PARTICIPLE
worn

CONDITIONAL

Conditional II

I	would	wear
you	would	wear
he/she/it	would	wear
we	would	wear
you	would	wear
they	would	wear

Conditional Past

I	would have	worn
you	would have	worn
he/she/it	would have	worn
we	would have	worn
you	would have	worn
they	would have	worn

WORK
trabalhar

SIMPLE

Present Simple

I work
you work
he/she/it works
we work
you work
they work

Past Simple

I worked
you worked
he/she/it worked
we worked
you worked
they worked

Present Perfect

I have worked
you have worked
he/she/it has worked
we have worked
you have worked
they have worked

Past Perfect

I had worked
you had worked
he/she/it had worked
we had worked
you had worked
they had worked

CONTINUOUS

Present Continuous

I am working
you are working
he/she/it is working
we are working
you are working
they are working

Past Continuous

I was working
you were working
he/she/it was working
we were working
you were working
they were working

Present Perfect Continuous

I have been working
you have been working
he/she/it has been working
we have been working
you have been working
they have been working

Past Perfect Continuous

I had been working
you had been working
he/she/it had been working
we had been working
you had been working
they had been working

FUTURE

Future I

I will work
you will work
he/she/it will work
we will work
you will work
they will work

Future I Continuous

I will be working
you will be working
he/she/it will be working
we will be working
you will be working
they will be working

Future II

I will have worked
you will have worked
he/she/it will have worked
we will have worked
you will have worked
they will have worked

Future II Continuous

I will have been working
you will have been working
he/she/it will have been working
we will have been working
you will have been working
they will have been working

IMPERATIVE
work

GERUND
working

PAST PARTICIPLE
worked

CONDITIONAL

Conditional II

I would work
you would work
he/she/it would work
we would work
you would work
they would work

Conditional Past

I would have worked
you would have worked
he/she/it would have worked
we would have worked
you would have worked
they would have worked

WRITE

escrever

+ *-ing* → ~~e~~ (ver p. 8)

SIMPLE

Present Simple

I	write
you	write
he/she/it	writes
we	write
you	write
they	write

Past Simple

I	wrote
you	wrote
he/she/it	wrote
we	wrote
you	wrote
they	wrote

Present Perfect

I	have	written
you	have	written
he/she/it	has	written
we	have	written
you	have	written
they	have	written

Past Perfect

I	had	written
you	had	written
he/she/it	had	written
we	had	written
you	had	written
they	had	written

CONTINUOUS

Present Continuous

I	am	writing
you	are	writing
he/she/it	is	writing
we	are	writing
you	are	writing
they	are	writing

Past Continuous

I	was	writing
you	were	writing
he/she/it	was	writing
we	were	writing
you	were	writing
they	were	writing

Present Perfect Continuous

I	have been	writing
you	have been	writing
he/she/it	has been	writing
we	have been	writing
you	have been	writing
they	have been	writing

Past Perfect Continuous

I	had been	writing
you	had been	writing
he/she/it	had been	writing
we	had been	writing
you	had been	writing
they	had been	writing

FUTURE

Future I

I	will	write
you	will	write
he/she/it	will	write
we	will	write
you	will	write
they	will	write

Future I Continuous

I	will be writing
you	will be writing
he/she/it	will be writing
we	will be writing
you	will be writing
they	will be writing

Future II

I	will have	written
you	will have	written
he/she/it	will have	written
we	will have	written
you	will have	written
they	will have	written

Future II Continuous

I	will have been	writing
you	will have been	writing
he/she/it	will have been	writing
we	will have been	writing
you	will have been	writing
they	will have been	writing

IMPERATIVE

write

GERUND

writing

PAST PARTICIPLE

written

CONDITIONAL

Conditional II

I	would	write
you	would	write
he/she/it	would	write
we	would	write
you	would	write
they	would	write

Conditional Past

I	would have	written
you	would have	written
he/she/it	would have	written
we	would have	written
you	would have	written
they	would have	written

Verbos irregulares

Infinitive **Infinitivo**	*Past Simple* **Pretérito**	*Past Participle* **Particípio passado**	*Portuguese* **Português**
be	was/were	been	ser, estar
beat	beat	beaten	bater
become	became	become	tornar-se
begin	began	begun	começar
bend	bent	bent	dobrar, curvar
bite	bit	bitten	morder
blow	blew	blown	soprar
break	broke	broken	quebrar
bring	brought	brought	trazer
build	built	built	construir
burn	burnt	burnt	queimar
buy	bought	bought	comprar
can	could	(been able)	poder
catch	caught	caught	agarrar
choose	chose	chosen	escolher
come	came	come	vir
cost	cost	cost	custar
cut	cut	cut	cortar
dig	dug	dug	escavar
do	did	done	fazer
draw	drew	drawn	desenhar
dream	dreamt	dreamt	sonhar
drink	drank	drunk	beber
drive	drove	driven	dirigir
eat	ate	eaten	comer
fall	fell	fallen	cair
feed	fed	fed	alimentar
feel	felt	felt	sentir
fight	fought	fought	lutar
find	found	found	achar
fly	flew	flown	voar
forecast	forecast(ed)	forecast(ed)	prever
forget	forgot	forgotten	esquecer
forgive	forgave	forgiven	perdoar
freeze	froze	frozen	congelar
get	got	got / IA: gotten	obter, contrair (doença)

give	gave	given	dar
go	went	gone	ir
grow	grew	grown	crescer
hang	hung	hung	pendurar
have	had	had	ter
hear	heard	heard	ouvir
hide	hid	hidden	esconder
hit	hit	hit	bater
hold	held	held	segurar
hurt	hurt	hurt	machucar
keep	kept	kept	manter
know	knew	known	conhecer, saber
lay	laid	laid	deitar
lead	led	led	conduzir
learn	learnt, learned	learnt, learned	aprender
leave	left	left	deixar, abandonar
lend	lent	lent	emprestar, pedir emprestado
let	let	let	deixar
lie	lay	lain	deitar-se
light	lit	lit	acender
lose	lost	lost	perder
make	made	made	fazer
may	might	–	dever, poder
meet	met	met	encontrar
must	(had to)	(had to)	precisar
pay	paid	paid	pagar
put	put	put	pôr
read	read	read	ler
ride	rode	ridden	cavalgar, andar (de veículo)
ring	rang	rung	tocar (campainha)
run	ran	run	correr
say	said	said	dizer
see	saw	seen	ver
sell	sold	sold	vender
send	sent	sent	enviar
shake	shook	shaken	chacoalhar
shine	shone	shone	brilhar
shoot	shot	shot	atirar

show	showed	shown	mostrar
shut	shut	shut	fechar
sing	sang	sung	cantar
sit	sat	sat	sentar
sleep	slept	slept	dormir
smell	smelt	smelt	cheirar
speak	spoke	spoken	falar
spell	spelt / spelled	spelt / spelled	soletrar
spend	spent	spent	despender
spill	spilt, spilled	spilt, spilled	derramar
spoil	spoilt, spoiled	spoilt, spoiled	estragar
stand	stood	stood	ficar em pé
steal	stole	stolen	roubar
stick	stuck	stuck	colar
sting	stung	stung	picar
swim	swam	swum	nadar
take	took	taken	pegar, tomar
teach	taught	taught	ensinar
tell	told	told	dizer, contar
think	thought	thought	pensar
throw	threw	thrown	jogar (fora)
understand	understood	understood	compreender
wake	woke	woken	acordar
wear	wore	worn	vestir
win	won	won	ganhar, vencer
write	wrote	written	escrever

Lista de verbos em ordem alfabética – Português-Inglês